Economics and Politics of Energy in the Middle East and Eastern Europe

Economics and Politics of Energy in the Middle East and Eastern Europe

Edited by
Natalya Ketenci and Ayşe Sevencan

LEXINGTON BOOKS
Lanham • Boulder • New York • London

Published by Lexington Books
An imprint of The Rowman & Littlefield Publishing Group, Inc.
4501 Forbes Boulevard, Suite 200, Lanham, Maryland 20706
www.rowman.com

6 Tinworth Street, London SE11 5AL, United Kingdom

British Library Cataloguing in Publication Information Available

Library of Congress Control Number: 2021934108

ISBN 978-1-7936-4447-3 (cloth)
ISBN 978-1-7936-4448-0 (electronic)

Contents

Introduction 1

1 Energy Map of Eastern Europe and the Middle East 5
Alper Altınanahtar

2 Energy Resources of the Eastern Mediterranean: The EastMed Project 15
Natalya Ketenci

3 Energy Efficiency and Human Development in Eastern Europe's Leading Energy Supplier Countries 23
Ayşe Sevencan

4 Search for Gaining Economic and Political Power without Any Resources 35
Levent Çağrı Uslu

5 Energy as a Complicating Factor: Conflict in the Eastern Mediterranean and the New Challenges in Cyprus Question 47
Gizem Alioğlu Çakmak and Melih Güner

6 Friends or Foes? Climate and Energy Policies in Turkey 83
Barış Gençer Baykan

7 Renewable Energy, Electricity Production, and Economic Growth in the Middle East 91
Gülfer Vural

8 Analysis of the Renewable Energy Sources for the Middle East Countries 99
Hatice Kerra Geldi

9 From Past to Future: The Entrepreneurial Ecosystem for Energy Start-ups in Turkey 115
Özlem Kunday

10 Sustainable Energy Supply Chain Management 129
Özlem Şenvar

Conclusion 139

Index 141

About the Editors and Contributors 145

Introduction

Energy issue was always important for the population to maintain and to advance technological progress and economic growth. The scope of energy discussions and concerns in the world expanded significantly in the last several decades. In order to cope with accelerating pollution from fossil fuels, countries increase investments in renewable energy power plants. However, the existing technology does not allow to increase significantly the capacity of renewable energy facilities in a short period; therefore, this process takes a relatively long time. One of the efficient solutions for renewable energy generation is nuclear power. However, some countries, particularly European countries, in order to decrease the risk of an accident, which consequences can be irreversible for the world, phase out their nuclear reactors. As a result, in order to maintain economic growth, countries continue to be highly dependent on fossil fuels such as oil, natural gas, and coal. At the same time, some countries start to encounter such problems as depletion of their oil and natural gas resources, for example, the United Kingdom. Consequently, new discoveries of fossil fuels in the world attract high international attention.

The aim of this book is to analyze energy resources in the Middle East and Eastern Europe and relations between countries that appear as a result of new discoveries in this area. The energy issues in this area are analyzed from different aspects in order to have a clear scope of possibilities and relations at regional and international levels. One of the striking features of this book is that it combines different aspects of energy issues in the Middle East and Eastern Europe and discusses possibilities for international cooperation at the political as well as economic levels.

This book consists of ten chapters, which can be organized into several themes. The First three chapters of the book are devoted to the overview of energy resources in the Middle East region, which attracts the attention of

Eastern Europe and the European Union. They focuse on geopolitical issues and include discussions on existing and possible cooperation between these two regions within the energy scope. The first chapter analyzes the energy map of Eastern Europe and the Middle East and compares these links to the world energy market. In the end, this chapter discusses the impact of the COVID-19 pandemic on energy markets in the scope of relations between the Middle East and Eastern Europe. The next chapter analyzes energy recourses in the Eastern Mediterranean, focusing on the EastMed project. This chapter analyzes the demand and supply of natural gas and oil in the European Union and the increasing level of import dependency. The possible routes of the EastMed projects are discussed, focusing on the route through Turkey and on issues that impede the possibilities for this route. The next chapter focuses on the major energy suppliers such as Russia, Iraq, Saudi Arabia, Norway, Kazakhstan, Nigeria, and Algeria to Europe. Relations between energy efficiency, economic growth, and human development of these suppliers are analyzed in this chapter.

The next two chapters are devoted to political cooperation and conflicts related to energy resources in the region. Chapter 4 analyzes how economic resources can help countries to gain political power in the example of Russia. At the same time, the chapter discusses, on the example of Turkey, how the absence of energy resources and suitable geographical location can create numerous advantages to a country, including political power. It also analyzes the role of Turkey in the "Energy Game" between Europe and the Middle East. Chapter 5 analyzes political relations between Turkey and Greece and focuses on the impact of the energy crisis on the bilateral relations of these two countries. It also discusses how the energy question in the East Mediterranean region started to function as a complicating factor in the traditional Cyprus question.

The next three chapters of the book is focusing on climate and renewable energy issues in the regions. Chapter 6 discusses climate change in the southern belt of Mediterranean Europe and Turkey. It analyzes the levels of climate and energy policies on climate change in Turkey and to what extent they are consistent with commitments and alignments in the European Union. Chapter 7 analyzes relations between renewable energy, electricity production, and economic growth in the Middle East in the scope of global warming. It focuses on renewable sources in Middle East countries as well and also studies the economic aspects of renewable energy capacity in the region despite their high potential in nonrenewable resources. Chapter 8 analyses renewable energy sources of the Middle East region. Electricity generation using sources like solar, wind, hydropower, and geothermal energy is examined. The author discusses possible investment opportunities in the renewable energy market in the Middle East region and conditions of the legal framework that guide countries towards a cleaner environment.

The last two chapters of the book analyze energy issues in the region from microeconomics points of view. Chapter 9 examines how the privatization and deregulations in the energy sector have opened opportunities for private companies and entrepreneurs in Turkey. Based on interviews with top-level managers of energy companies, investors as well as founders of energy start-ups located in Istanbul, this chapter provides valuable insights for entrepreneurs intending to enter the energy sector.

The last chapter concludes with the analysis of the supply chain. It also provides an overview of sustainable energy supply chain management. The focus of this chapter is an extension of supply chain management concepts to address the challenges of energy management.

Keywords: Middle East, Eastern Europe, Energy Issue, Natural Gas and Oil, Turkey

Chapter 1

Energy Map of Eastern Europe and the Middle East

Alper Altınanahtar

ABSTRACT

The world has already entered almost a quarter century into the second millennia. Things have been changing incredibly fast, and the biggest contributor to this speed is the discovery of electricity and the vast use of renewable and nonrenewable energy sources. The Middle East undoubtedly owns the largest crude oil reserves, while Eastern European countries have alternative sources of energy. In this chapter, we will first explain all sources of energy while drawing an energy map for Eastern Europe and the Middle East. Later, we will establish their places in the world energy market in terms of usage and supply of all sources of energy. The chapter will also provide some brief information in regard to these countries' future plans in energy supply, usage, and more importantly their potential impact on climate change. Finally, due to the current pandemic around the world, a small section of this chapter will be devoted to the impact of COVID-19 pandemic on energy markets, especially in Eastern Europe and in the Middle East.

Keywords: Energy Map, Eastern Europe, Middle East, Energy Sources, Energy Supply, COVID-19 and Energy

INTRODUCTION

There are two main categories of energy sources: carbon-based fossil fuel and alternatives. Fossil fuel mainly comes in three different forms: petroleum (or oil is a term that includes products such as crude oil and diesel), coal (one of the most abundant fossil fuels), and natural gas. Alternative energy sources come in two different forms: renewables and nonrenewables. Renewable energy sources include sources such as solar, wind, hydro, and geothermal, and nonrenewables include sources such as nuclear power and biofuels.

According to World 101 (2020) in 2017, while the most commonly used energy sources (85% of the total) were coal, natural gas, and oil, followed by renewable energy, mainly hydroelectricity (10%) and nuclear energy, countries consumed a different mix of energy sources. Most of the Middle Eastern countries relied mostly on oil, while countries such as Norway and Sweden are almost completely reliant on hydropower for their grids (IHA, 2020). These differences aroused due to three main reasons: economic needs, natural resources of the country, and environmental concerns.[1.]

In this chapter, two regions, Eastern Europe and the Middle East, will be investigated and compared. Various sources define the borders of the Middle East differently. For instance, Britannica (2020) considers Turkey, Libya, Sudan, etc. as a part of the Middle East, whereas according to the International Energy Agency (IEA) Middle East is comprised of the following 12 countries: Bahrain, Iran, Iraq, Jordan, Kuwait, Lebanon, Oman, Qatar, Saudi Arabia, Syria, United Arab Emirates (UAE and their total GDP in 2010 dollars adds up to $3.298 billion, although there are not many), and Yemen, with a total population of 237 million people. In 2010 dollars, their total GDP adds up to $2,368 billion (International Energy Agency, 2019). On the other hand, there is a consensus on the Eastern European countries. As defined by the United Nations Statistics Division (1999), there are ten Eastern European countries, namely, Belarus, Bulgaria, Czechia, Hungary, Moldova, Poland, Romania, Russia, Slovakia, and Ukraine. These countries have a total population of 290 million similarities between the two regions; they both play a significant role in the global energy market and energy trade. Only major players among these countries will be analyzed in detail, while others will only be mentioned by their regional contributions.

The next section will outline the main energy sources and the output of these energy types in these two regions. Section 3will focus on the Middle East's and Eastern Europe's energy consumption. In section 4, the impact of environmental concerns on these two regions' energy production and consumption will be discussed. Section 5 will shed some light on the energy markets given the current coronavirus pandemic around the world and its effect on the energy market, and in section 6 we will conclude.

SOURCES AND SUPPLY OF ENERGY

Sources of Energy

According to EIA (2020) and BP Statistical Review of World Energy (2020), Russia has the largest natural gas reserves (19.1% of the world reserves) in the world and it is followed by Iran (16.1%), Qatar (12.4%, third), Saudi

Arabia (3.01%, fifth), UAE (2.98%, seventh), and Iraq (1.78%, twelfth). In Eastern Europe, Russia is followed by Ukraine and Romania. However, compared to Russia their shares are less than 1% of the world reserves, whereas in the Middle East ten out of twelve countries' natural gas reserves are greater than 0.1% of the total world reserves. Overall, Eastern Europe owns 19.7% and the Middle East owns 37.8 % of natural gas reserves. With current extraction rates, Eastern Europe will likely drain its reserves in about 50 years. In the Middle East, on the other hand, natural gas reserves will likely last well over a century (BP Statistical Review of World Energy, 2020).

According to the latest data provided by BP Statistical Review of World Energy (2020), the Middle Eastern countries own 48.1% of the oil reserves in the world, and more than half of these reserves (26.2%) are located in Saudi Arabia and Iran. Eastern Europe, on the other hand, owns only a little bit over 6% of the world oil reserves and almost all of it is located in Russia. Less than 0.05% of the world oil reserves are located in Romania. If production remains constant in these countries, oil reserves will last between 20 and 25 years, while reserves in Saudi Arabia and Iran will last 69 and 120 years, respectively. For other Middle Eastern countries, it will last anywhere between 15 and 291 years. These extreme values are either due to very low production levels (i.e., Syria) or the mount of reserves (i.e., Oman).

In terms of coal, Eastern Europe is much luckier than the Middle East. A little bit over 0.1% of the world coal reserves is located in the Middle East, while 21.7% of the world coal reserves are located in Eastern Europe, of which 15.2% is in Russia. At the current extraction rate reserves in Russia will last over 350 years (BP Statistical Review of World Energy, 2020).

Geothermal, solar, hydro, and wind power construe the renewable part of alternative energy while nuclear power and biofuel construe the nonrenewable part of alternative energy. In 2019 cumulative installed geothermal power capacity in Eastern Europe was 0.53%, all based in Russia, whereas the Middle East has no geothermal power worth mentioning. Cumulative installed photovoltaic (PV) power (solar power), on the other hand, is an area that's more than three folded over the past three years in the Middle East. Especially in UAE, solar power capacity has grown 217.2% from 2018 to 2019. Still, the total share of the Middle East corresponds to less than 1% of the total world solar power capacity. From 2018 to 2019 Eastern Europe's solar power capacity share has increased from 1.7% to 2.3% of the world cumulative installed solar power. Most of this increase can be attributed to Ukraine, Russia, and Hungary, with a rise in their solar power capacity of 196.4%, 98.7%, and 75.9%, respectively.

As expected, due to environmental factors, hydroelectricity generation in the Middle East is meaningful only in Iran and Iraq. Their share in the world is 0.69% and 0.06%, and between 2018 and 2019 Iran increased its capacity by 154.3%. The rest of the Middle East has a share of less than 0.05% of the world's hydroelectricity generation, while Eastern Europe, on the other hand, has a share of 5.3%. The major part of this capacity is located in Russia (4.6%), followed by Romania (0.36%), Slovakia (0.1%), and Bulgaria (0.08%). The rest of the countries in Eastern Europe contribute less than 0.05% of the world's hydroelectricity production.

Cumulative installed wind turbine capacity in the world increased from 17.304 to 622.704 megawatts between 2000 and 2019. In 2000, both Eastern Europe and Middle Eastern regions contributed to the world capacity by less than 0.07% each. In 2019, however, Eastern Europe's share increased to 1.76% and the Middle East's share increased to 11%. Between 2018 and 2019, Russia and Ukraine both doubled their installed wind turbine while the capacity was seen in Jordan by 30%. Although both regions' contribution to world's installed wind turbine capacity in Eastern Europe, whereas in the Middle East the biggest increase in installed wind turbine capacity remains relatively small. Eastern Europe has increased its capacity by 918 times while the Middle East by 60 times. Both regions growth rates are way above the growth rate of world installed wind turbine capacity between 2000 and 2019.

Until 2011, the Middle East did not have any nuclear power generation and since then the only country that produces nuclear power in the region is Iran. In 2017 Iran reached its peak levels of 6.95 terawatt-hours from 0.1 terawatt-hours in 2011. In the following two years, however, its output went down to 6.41 terawatt-hours. Even at Iran's peak levels of nuclear power generation, regions' share of the world output remained around 0.002%. Eastern Europe, on the other hand, was much more experienced in nuclear power generation. During the same time period, between 2011 and 2019, Eastern Europe expanded its output by 9% while the world total nuclear power production increased by only 5.45%. In 2019, regions' total output was almost 14% of the total world nuclear power output. As expected, Russia is the leader with a 7.5% share of the total world output. As mentioned in the previous section, the ranking of these two regions' countries reveals their importance in the global energy markets.

Energy Supply

Here, the Total Primary Energy Supply (TPES), by source, in countries disposals will be reported. For consistency and simplicity in comparison IEA's scale of energy measurement which is kiloton of oil equivalent (ktoe) will be used. ktoe is a unit of energy defined as the amount of energy released by burning one thousand tons of crude oil. The data provided in this part of the study was gathered from International Energy Agency (2019).

In 2017, TPES of Iran was the largest in the Middle East at 261.608 ktoe and 174.574 ktoe of that came from natural gas and followed by Saudi Arabia with 21.321 ktoe of total energy and 78.009 ktoe of it came from natural gas. However, TPES attributed to oil in Saudi Arabia was the highest with 133.291 ktoe, followed by Iran with 82.356 ktoe. These two countries have supplied more than 60% of the total primary energy in the region by using more than 60% of the natural gas and more than 66% of the oil in the Middle East. Other sources of energy in the Middle East add up to only 1.16% of the total energy supply of the Middle East. The only nuclear power producer in the region is Iran, with 1.958 ktoe (BP Statistical Review of World Energy, 2020).

For the same year in Eastern Europe, Russia was the biggest total energy supplier with 733.071 ktoe. The biggest share belonged to natural gas with 388.334 ktoe, the second-biggest share to oil with 153.963 ktoe, and the third-biggest share to coal with 113.581 ktoe. Russia happens to be the greatest supplier of natural gas, oil, and coal in Eastern Europe. In total energy supply, Poland came second with 103.845 ktoe, and Ukraine was the third biggest with 89.462 ktoe energy suppliers in the region (BP Statistical Review of World Energy, 2020).

Based on data gathered from BP Statistical Review of World Energy (2020), the Middle East not only possesses the largest oil reserves in the world but also produces the most in the world. Thirty-two percent of the oil supply in the world comes from Middle Eastern countries. Saudi Arabia alone is responsible for 12% of the world oil supply, which is greater than the total Eastern Europe's oil production. Even though Russia is the second-largest oil producer in the world, the rest of the region's countries contribution to oil production is less than Yemen's oil production. Regions' oil production share in the world is only 12%. Due to sanctions over Iran, most of these reserves are used for domestic purposes (primary fuel source, 70%, for electricity) and the rest is sold to Turkey (73% of total natural gas exports), Armenia, Azerbaijan, and Iraq via pipelines unless there are some technical problems. EIA (2020) reveals that in 2017 the greatest oil importer from Iran was China, followed by India, Turkey, and South Korea. Although Iran has a huge potential of becoming an energy supplier to Europe, prevailing embargo conditions due to Iran's nuclear program, between 2012 and 2016, EIA (2020) has prevented investments in Iran's gas and oil industries. From 2018 to 2019, Iran's oil production went down by 26.4%. All upstream oil and natural gas projects are managed by the state-owned National Iranian Company (EIA, 2020). Although foreign or private ownership of natural resources is prohibited by the Iranian constitution, recent developments now allow international private oil companies to participate in the finding and developing phases through the Iranian petroleum contract.

With its significant oil (second) and natural gas (fifth) reserves in the world, Saudi Arabia remains the world's dominant oil exporter. Iraq, on the other hand, unlike Saudi Arabia, due to deterioration in its political stability and security could not become a major player in the oil and natural gas market. Most gas is either used for domestic power production or flared/reinjected. However, Iran and Iraq are the two Middle Eastern countries, which have maintained their production growth due to their vast proven reserves and low extraction costs. Although UAE is ranked among the first ten countries with the largest oil and gas reserves, the country has been a net importer of gas in the last few years. The gas is mainly reinjected in oil reserves and also used for domestic power (Dreyer, Stang, Mandil, & Handerson, 2014). Contrary to its geographical size, Kuwait was the ninth-largest oil producer in the world. On the other hand, after United States being the second natural gas producer in the world, Russia's total gas production (17% of world's total production) is almost equal to the Middle East's total (17.4% of the world's total production).

Coal is one of the energy resources that the Middle East lacks, with less than 0.05% of the world production. Eastern Europe, on the other hand, Russia leading with 5.4% of world production, is responsible for 8.2% of the world's coal production. The interesting thing about coal between 2018 and 2019 is that while its production has not changed over the world, the Eastern Europe's coal production has shrunk by 4.5%. Bulgaria decreased its production by 50%, Hungary by 13.3%, Poland and Romania by over 8%, Czechia by 6.4%, and Russia by 0.3% during the same time period.

ENERGY USAGE

According to BP Statistical Review of World Energy (2020) report in 2019, Russia was the fourth-largest primary energy consumer in the world, Iran the 10th, Saudi Arabia the 11th, UAE the 22nd, Poland the 24th, and Ukraine the 32nd. The world ranking of other Eastern European and Middle Eastern countries remained below 40. Russia being the largest primary energy consumer in Eastern Europe uses natural gas (54%), oil (22%), coal (12%), nuclear (6%), and hydroelectric (6%) as the source of its energy consumption. Other Eastern European countries such as Poland depend mostly on coal (44%), oil (31%), and natural gas (17%). Ukraine depends mostly on coal (32%) and natural gas (30%). Whereas for Iran, sources of primary energy consumption was natural gas (65%), followed by oil (31%).

The Middle East's share in the total world's oil consumption is 9.5%, which is 80% more than the Eastern Europe's, and, as expected, Russia in Eastern Europe and Saudi Arabia in the Middle East are the biggest oil consumers. Both regions' natural gas consumption in 2019 was very close to each other; Eastern Europe's share was 13.9%, and the Middle East's share was 14.2% of the world's total natural gas consumption. Russia was responsible for the consumption of almost 81% of the total natural gas consumed in Eastern Europe, whereas in the Middle East the majority of natural gas was consumed by Iran and Saudi Arabia. Unlike other Middle Eastern countries, Jordan does not have significant amounts of energy resources. Hence, the country mostly relies on imports of crude oil and natural gas from its neighbors. As the last carbon-based fossil fuel, coal is one of the least consumed sources of energy in these two regions and due to limited resources in the Middle East, the region has a share only quarter of a 1% of the world's total coal consumption while Eastern Europe's share is 0.05%.

Compared to Eastern Europe, nuclear power consumption is insignificant in the Middle East for obvious reasons. Eastern Europe consumes 13.6% of the world's nuclear power, while the Middle East consumes only one-fifth of a 1% of the world's nuclear power. Biofuel is consumed mostly in Poland, which is 1% of the world's total. However, between 2018 and 2019, Poland's biofuel consumption increased by 6.7%.

Renewable energy usage in Eastern Europe, except Russia and Ukraine, increased by less than 15% between 2018 and 2019. In fact, in Slovakia, it decreased by 13%. Russia and Ukraine increased their consumption of renewable energy by 31% and 92.4%, respectively. The Middle Eastern countries' interest in renewable energy consumption for the same time period was much greater. In Saudi Arabia, its consumption has increased by 365.6%, in UAE by 214.8%, and in Kuwait by 91.4%. Most of this increase in the Middle East can be attributed to the increase in the use of solar energy. For Eastern European countries, most of the increase in renewable energy use can be attributed to the solar power as well, but in the region wind power usage has also increased significantly, especially in Ukraine, Russia, Poland, and the Czech Republic.

CONTRIBUTION TO CLIMATE CHANGE—CO_2 EMISSIONS

In the last few decades, countries have realized the importance of global warming and how the future of the world depends on today's actions more than ever. Among many others, CO_2 emissions are known to be one of the most important factors contributing the global warming. In fact, NASA (2020) describes CO_2 as "the most important long-lived 'forcing' of climate change."

Eastern Europe contributed 6.9%, while the Middle East contributed 6.3% to the world CO_2 emissions in 2019 (BP Statistical Review of World

Energy, 2020). Russia alone was responsible for almost 65% of the total CO_2 emissions in Eastern Europe, followed by Poland 12.8% and Ukraine 7.8%. Other countries' contribution to the region's CO_2 emissions remained below 4%. In the Middle East, Iran has contributed to the CO_2 emissions the most, 30%, followed by Saudi Arabia, 26.7%, and UAE, 13%. Other countries' contribution to the region's CO_2 emissions remained below 7%. Over the past decade, between 2010 and 2019, all Eastern European countries have reduced their CO_2 emissions between 35% (Ukraine) and 2% (Belarus). The only country that failed to reduce its CO_2 emissions was Russia. Its CO_2 emissions went up by 3% between 2010 and 2019. The reduction in CO_2 emissions in Eastern Europe was clearly a result of the European Union's 2030 targets of reduced greenhouse gas emissions. These targets require cutbacks on the use of coal and substituting gas and renewables instead (Winrow, 2016). Middle Eastern countries, on the other hand, were way far away from meeting similar requirements. CO_2 emissions increased between 12%, Kuwait, and 77%, Oman, in the same period. Saudi Arabia, the second-largest contributor to CO_2 emissions in the region, decided to reduce the use of fossil fuels in its electricity sector by at least 50% by 2020 to use them for export (Vakhshouri, 2015; Dreyer, Stang, Mandil, & Handerson, 2014). Even though country's CO_2 emissions significantly increased between 2010 and 2019 after 2016 there was a slight decrease in the country's CO_2 emissions.

COVID-19 IMPACT ON ENERGY MARKET

One of the most comprehensive and most cited reports in regard to COVID-19's impact on energy markets around the world was published by International Energy Agency (2020). According to the reports, the first impact of COVID-19 was forcing countries to either a partial or a complete lockdown, which resulted in a decrease in weekly energy demand between 18% and 25% on average. As a result, there was a decline in the global energy demand in the first quarter of 2020 by 3.8% which is expected to decrease up to 6% if lockdowns and restrictions on mobility and commercial activities continue in 2020. Except renewables, the global demand for coal, oil, and gas were all decreased by 8%, 5%, and 2%, respectively. Shutting down the commercial and industrial operations and limited mobility and restrictions in aviation were the main reasons for the shrinking of these energy markets. By April 2020, the price of Brent crude per barrel had fallen to its lowest level since November 2002 (Dutta, Das, Jana, & Vo, 2020). The only good outcome of COVID-19 pandemic may be the decline in global CO_2 emissions. In the first quarter of 2020, the global CO_2 emissions were 5% lower than the first quarter's global CO_2 emissions of 2019 and expected to decline up to 8% by the end of 2020.

CONCLUSION

Based on the descriptive statistics provided in the previous sections, one can easily infer that in terms of energy sources, production and consumption Eastern Europe is dominated by Russia (Goldthau, 2015). On the other hand, in the Middle East, except Jordan, Lebanon, and Yemen, others have vast sources of energy. Although Russia has remained as one of the biggest producers and exporters of energy over the years, Blumenthal and Scissors (2015) claim that Russia's major role is at risk. On the other hand, countries like Iran and Iraq in the Middle East can be game changers if they could elevate their political challenges and by 2030 Middle East energy production is expected to grow by 33% (Vakhshouri, 2015). However, according to EIA, only to maintain its current global market share for another fifteen years, the Middle East needs $3.7 trillion of investment in its energy sector.

NOTE

1. In 2016, 185 countries pledged to increase their use of clean energy as part of the Paris Agreement, a treaty that allowed signatories to set their own goals for lower carbon emissions.

REFERENCES

Blumenthal, D., & Scissors, D. M. (Eds.). (2015). *Too Much Energy? Asia at 2030*. American Enterprise Institute.

BP Statistical Review of World Energy. (2020). Statistical Review of World Energy 69th ed. Retrieved July 25, 2020, from https://www.bp.com/: https://www.bp.com/en/global/corporate/energy-economics/statistical-review-of-world-energy.html.

Britannica. (2020, July). Retrieved from Britannica.com: https://www.britannica.com/place/Middle-East.

Dreyer, I., Stang, G., Mandil, C., & Handerson, J. (2014). *Energy moves and power shifts. The Geopolitics of Energy*. Paris: European Union Institute for Security Studies (EUISS). Retrieved from https://www.jstor.org/stable/resrep07072.6.

Dutta, A., Das, D., Jana, R., & Vo, X. V. (2020). COVID-19 and oil market crash: Revisiting the Safe haven property of gold and Bitcoin. *Resources Policy*. doi: https://doi.org/10.1016/j.resourpol.2020.101816.

EIA. (2013, July). *Iran Country Analysis Brief*. Energy Information Administration.

EIA. (2020, July). *Country Analysis Brief: Iran. U.S. Energy Information Administration.* Retrieved from US Energy Information Administration.

Goldthau, A. (2015). The Russian Energy Outlook. In D. Blumenthal, & D. M. Scissors (Eds.), *Too Much Energy? Asia at 2030* (pp. 51–60). American Enterprise Institute.

IHA. (2020, May). REGION: Europe. Retrieved from International Hydropower Association: https://www.hydropower.org/country-profiles/region-europe.

International Energy Agency. (2019). IEA World Energy Balances 2019. IEA. Retrieved from https://www.iea.org/reports/world-energy-balances-2019.

International Energy Agency. (2020). Global Energy Review 2020—The Impacts of the Covid-19 Crisis on Global Energy Demand and CO_2 Emissions. Retrieved July 30, 2020, from https://www.iea.org/reports/global-energy-review-2020.

NASA. (2020). The Causes of Climate Change. Retrieved July 25, 2020, from NASA: https://climate.nasa.gov/causes/.

United Nations Statistics Division. (1999). Standard country or area codes for statistical use (M49). Retrieved from United Nations: https://unstats.un.org/unsd/methodology/m49/.

Vakhshouri, S. (2015). The Middle East Energy Outlook. In D. Blumenthal, & D. M. Scissors (Eds.), *Too Much Energy? Asia at 2030* (pp. 41–50). American Enterprise Institute.

Winrow, G. M. (2016). The European Energy Landscape. In T. Harry, F. Hubert, & A. G. Moran (Ed.), *Global Energy Debates and the Eastern Mediterranean* (pp. 15–21). Atlantic Council. Retrieved from https://www.jstor.org/stable/resrep17091.6.

World 101. (2020). Sources of Energy; A Comparison. Retrieved June 15, 2020, from World101: https://world101.cfr.org/global-era-issues/climate-change/sources-energy-comparison.

Chapter 2

Energy Resources of the Eastern Mediterranean

The EastMed Project

Natalya Ketenci

ABSTRACT

Nonrenewable resources are limited; therefore, countries worldwide attempt to decrease dependence on them and increase the production of renewable energy sources. However, there is a long way to reverse this dependency. In 2018, the share of nonrenewable sources in total energy consumption of the world composed 84.7%, which declined from 86.82% in 2000 and from 91.62% in 1980 (BP, 2018). Therefore, until new technologies are invented to significantly increase renewable energy production and to increase energy productivity (efficiency), international attention will continue to concentrate around new promising discoveries of nonrenewable energy sources. One such discovery is located in the Eastern Mediterranean area, which attracts not only the interest of neighboring countries but particularly international interest, due to its promising potential. The purpose of this chapter is to analyze the economic potential of new discoveries in the Eastern Mediterranean region in terms of benefits for the EU. In addition, this chapter discusses economic efficiency and possibilities for the natural gas pipeline infrastructure in this region.

Keywords: The EastMed Project, Natural Gas, Levant Basin, Tamar field, Energy of Turkey

INTRODUCTION

Nowadays Eastern Mediterranean energy sources are associated with the Levant Basin Province, which covers approximately 83,000 km^2 of the

Eastern Mediterranean area, including offshore and onshore areas. The Levant Basin Province enters the exclusive economic zones of Cyprus, Egypt, Israel, Lebanon, and Syria. Discoveries and the production of energy resources started a quite long time ago in the region; however, its energy resources received international attention only less than a decade ago. The exploration of oil in Egypt takes origin in the 1860s, with its first discovered oil in the Gensa Field in 1869. However, production of oil was only possible in 1909 by the Anglo-Egyptian Oil Fields, a partnership between Royal Dutch Shell and Anglo-Persian Oil Company, which is known today as British Petroleum (Hurt, 2014), while the production of natural gas in Egypt for the commercial purposes started only in March 1967 (El Ayouty, 1985). Israel had its first discoveries of gas fields in 1993 and later in 2000 next to the Gaza Strip; however, they did not receive international consideration due to their unimportant size (Abu Gosh and Leal-Arcas, 2013).

There are several relatively new natural gas discoveries that attract international attention. The discovery in the Tamar gas field took place in 2008 and started to produce natural gas already in March of 2013. The discovery in the Leviathan gas field took place in 2010, where production has not commenced yet but is expected soon. At the time of discovery, the Tamar field was the largest gas field in the region, and it is the largest discovery of the Noble Energy, operating company in the field. The discovery in Leviathan gas field outperformed the Tamar field estimated reserves. These two gas fields are located very close to each other; the Tamar field is located off the coast of Israel, approximately 80 km west of Haifa city, while the Leviathan gas field is located 130 km west of Haifa. However, in 2015 the largest discovery in the region was made in the Zohr gas field, off the coast of Egypt, with an estimated 30 trillion cubic feet.

According to the United States Geological Survey 2010 estimations, the Levant Basin Province has around 1.7 billion barrels of technically recoverable oil and approximately 122 trillion cubic feet (3.45 trillion cubic meters) of recoverable gas. The estimated reserves of the Tamar gas field are about 318 billion cubic meters of natural gas and about 14.6 million barrels of oil. Estimations of the discovery in the Leviathan gas field are approximately 18 trillion cubic feet (509 billion cubic meters) and about 600 million barrels of oil bellow the gas layer. The operator of these two gas fields is the Noble Energy company, US, with the share of 39.66% in the Leviathan project and 25% in the Tamar project. In the Leviathan project, partners are Delek Group (Delek Drilling and Avner Oil Exploration) with 45.34% working interest and Ratio Oil Exploration with other stockholders having 15% of shares. In the Tamar field, the partner with the largest share is Isramco, 28.75%; Delek Drilling, 22%; Tamar Petroleum, 16.75%; Dor Gas Exploration, 4%; and Everest, 3.5% (Schenk et al. 2010).

THE EASTMED PROJECT

In February 2018, Delek Group, together with Noble Energy, signed an agreement with a private company, Dolphinus Holding, Egypt, for exporting natural gas from Leviathan and Tomar projects to Egypt. The approximate annual quantity of supply consists of approximately 3.5 billion cubic meters of natural gas from every field with the total contract quantity of approximately 32 billion cubic meters from every field, composing estimated total revenue of $15 billion.

On the other side, in 2017, the Ministry for Energy of Israel signed a joint venture Declaration with Italy, Greece, and Cyprus to confirm the support for the development of the EastMed pipeline project. The EastMed project is planned to connect natural gas extracted in Lavant Basin with the planned Poseidon multisource natural gas interconnector in Greece, which is stretching from the Turkish–Greek border to Italy, passing through Cyprus and Crete, and finally end in Italy. The planned length of the EastMed pipeline is 1,900 km, where 1,300 km is planned to be constructed underwater (offshore) and the rest 600 km onshore, which will pass through Greece. The final destination of the natural gas through the EastMed pipeline is Italy, after which it can continue through existing pipelines to other destinations in Europe.

The preparation stage of the project has gained two grants from the EU Connecting Europe Facility program; first worth 2,000,000 EUR was received in 2015 for the technical feasibility, economic, financial, and competitiveness studies to provide necessary information to contributors of the project by March 2018. Second grant has been received under the same program, worth 34,500,000 EUR, which is 50% of the cost of carrying the technical studies necessary for the starting the implementation stage of the project. The output of the study, by the end of 2021, has to provide the necessary information for finalizing the project route, project costs, and technical specifications required for tendering the construction stage of the project. However, the agreement for the construction of the EastMed project was quickly signed on January 2, 2020, between governments of Cyprus, Greece, and Israel with the plan to supply around 12 billion cubic meters of natural gas to Greece and later to Italy and further. According to Alex Lagakos, the deputy director of the Greek Energy Forum, the initial estimated cost of the project is around 6.7 billion US dollars (Papadimitrou, 2020). The support of the EU for the project illustrates the wish of the EU to decrease its dependence on the natural gas supplies from Russia, which makes Russia anxious as it plans to increase its export to the EU through new close to the finish TurkStream pipeline (31.5 billion cubic meters annually) and Nord Stream 2 (55 billion cubic meters annually) in addition to existing Nord Stream (55 billion cubic meters annually), Blue Stream (16 billion cubic meters annually), and Trans Balkan (14 billion cubic meters annually) gas pipelines. In 2018, about 40% of natural gas imports were from Russia, 35% from Norway, 11% from Algeria, and the rest from other countries (Eurostat).

THE EU'S VIEW

Natural gas is a strategic product for most of the countries in the world due to its scarcity and involvement in almost all industrial productions and households' consumption. The scarcity of natural gas makes countries' economies dependent on their imports, particularly countries with low level or no production of natural gas. For the past decade, the EU experienced a decline in the natural gas consumption by 11.24% in 2018 compared to 2008, with the deepest fall in 2014 by 22% compared to 2008 (Sönnichsen, 2020).

However, it is worth mentioning that the interest of the EU in the EastMed pipeline project is mainly based not on the consumption statistics but on the increasing energy dependency rate of European countries. For the past two decades, production of primary energy in the EU was in general decreasing, particularly the production of oil and natural gas has the deepest decline (Eurostat, 2019). Thus, the production of oil in the EU fell by 56.8% for the period 2000–2018, declining from 3.5 to 1.5 million barrels per day, where the main reason is a decline in the resource of the biggest EU oil producer, UK. For the same reason the production of natural gas in Europe dropped by 53.2% for the last two decades, declining from 233.5 to 109.2 billion cubic meters in 2018. The total primary energy production is expected to decrease for the period 2010–2050, with a higher rate relative to consumption (Ruble, 2017). Accordingly, the energy dependency of the EU continues and is expected to increase. In 2018, the energy dependency rate of the EU, on average, was 58% compared to 56% in 2000 (Eurostat, 2020).

Starting from 1991, European countries actively promote an increase in the production of renewable energy resources to protect the environment and to decrease dependency on scarce nonrenewable energy resources. Renewable energy directives are updated on a regularly basis and include goals for an increase in the renewable energy usage. Thus in 1997, the EU announced a target of 12% share of renewable sources in energy production by 2010. In 2009 this target was updated to 20% by 2020, which almost reached 18.9% in 2018. Apparently, targets compose an average for the EU, where all countries have individual targets relative to their initial conditions and existing possibilities for an increase in capacity. Thus the 2020 target for Malta was 10%, while it composed 49% for Sweden. In 2018, the average goal for the EU is updated to 32% by 2030 (EC, 2020).

Despite renewable energy policies directed on the increase in renewable resources production, the European countries one by one started to take a decision to decline or completely phase-out nuclear power. This tendency especially increased after the nuclear power plant accident in Japan in 2011. Germany, for example, was one of the ten largest producers of the nuclear power in the world, phased out eight out of its seventeen nuclear reactors with the succeeding shutting of the rest of the reactors by 2022. Belgium has planned to shut down seven active nuclear reactors by 2025, which are used in the generation of half of the country's electricity. It is planned to shut down seven nuclear reactors as well, in Spain, by 2030, which are involved in the generation of 20% of electricity in the country. By 2018, Italy and Lithuania closed all previously active nuclear reactors (Ketenci, 2019). A substantial decline in the nuclear power production is a sign of an increase in the demand for natural gas and the European countries' import dependence in the near future, as the renewable energy production has significant limitations in its growth.

As a result, despite an increase in energy production from renewable sources, the lag between domestic production of nonrenewable energy resources and their consumption continues to grow, which increases the energy dependency of European countries. To maintain energy security, it is essential for the European countries to diversify suppliers, where Russia is the main supplier of oil, 30% of total crude oil imports, natural gas, 40%, and coal, 42% (Eurostat, 2020). The diversification of energy suppliers will increase the level of competitiveness affecting the energy prices and reduce the risk of supply cuts in the case of political conflicts.

THE ROLE OF TURKEY

There are a lot of discussions around the EastMed pipeline project, which exclude Turkey and TRNC, despite the planned routes to pass through territorial waters of Turkey. However, this is not the only reason for discussions around the planned project. Another matter is the declining demand for natural gas in Europe. According to the British Petroleum Statistical Review of World Energy for the period 2008–2017, consumption of natural gas in Turkey increased by 46.2% in total, composing 5.2% average annual growth, which is the highest growth rate compared to European countries, however, with the sharp decline of about 8% in 2018. In general, statistics illustrate an increasing tendency of natural gas consumption in Turkey, while European countries experience decline, in general. For the last decade, only Austria, Germany, Greece, Norway, Poland, Portugal, and Switzerland experienced an increase in natural gas consumption with the highest 3.7% average annual growth rate in Portugal, which is significantly lower than in Turkey, while other European countries experienced an annual decline for the past decade. Though Greece experienced an average annual growth for the last decade, its natural gas consumption consists of one-tenth of consumption in Turkey. Italy's natural gas consumption exceeded Turkish consumption by about 46%; however, total natural gas consumption has declined by 14.5% for the last decade.

Natural gas infrastructure is capital intensive and requires a market with high potential. On the country-level, only Germany, Italy, and United Kingdom, out of European countries, had higher levels of natural gas consumption in 2018 compared to Turkey.

Turkey, which is excluded from negotiations, may become the last piece in the puzzle, where natural gas demand continuously grows. Turkey is an established energy hub due to its central geographic location and its continuous growth in energy demand. It has already developed natural gas infrastructure and at the same time continues with projects under construction like TANAP and the TurkStream. Usage of existing and constructing pipeline infrastructure for transporting natural gas from the Levant Basin may significantly decrease construction costs and completion period of the project and increase its efficiency in terms of capital returns. Despite these advantages, with the support of the European Union and the United States, the agreement for the construction of the EastMed project is signed between governments of Cyprus, Greece, and Israel. However, still the signing of the agreement does not provide a guaranty of the construction start, which is not economically efficient at this moment.

One of the reasons, the EU excluding Turkey from negotiations of the projects, is the fear that Turkey can use the project as a tool for manipulation in order to access the EU (Troulis, 2019). Another reason, which is important for the project and at the same time creates complications for its implementation, is the political conflict between Cyprus and Turkey. Turkey officially does not recognize the Republic of Cyprus, and requests to consider interests of all coastal states that are involved in the geopolitics of the project.

CONCLUSION

The depletion of oil and gas resources in European countries creates a need for the search for new energy resources. An increase in production and productivity of renewable resources takes a long time and requires continuing advances in technology. Therefore, the only solution for this period is to import nonrenewable resources. For example, Russia is ready to increase its supplies to Europe by constructing new additional pipeline networks to connect with Europe. However, in order to maintain energy security and to decrease energy dependency on one particular country, the EU is in search of additional suppliers. The new discoveries in the Eastern Mediterranean area attract the EU investors. The solution seems ideal for the EU; however, there are a lot of questions that need to be resolved before the EastMed project can take its start, where one of them is the Cyprus issue with Turkey. This project is possible and visible without passing the territory of Turkey; however, in this case, the cost of the project significantly increases by decreasing its efficiency. Before the project starts its construction and supplies its first natural gas, the EU dependency on Russian energy sources will continue to grow.

REFERENCES

Abu Gosh, E.S. and R. Leal-Arcas (2013). Gas and oil explorations in the Levant Basin: The case of Lebanon and Israel. *Oil, Gas & Energy Law Intelligence*, 11(3): 2–32.

BP (2018) Statistical Review of World Energy. http://www.bp.com/statisticalreview.

British Petroleum Statistical Review of World Energy EC, European Commission (2020). Renewable Energy Directive. Retrieved from: https://ec.europa.eu/energy/topics/renewable-energy/renewable-energy-directive/overview_en.

El Ayouty, M.K. (1985). Natural gas development in Egypt. *Energy*, 10(2), 227–230. Eurostat statistics.

Eurostat (2019). Energy statistics—an overview. Retrieved from: https://ec.europa.eu/eurostat/statistics-explained/pdfscache/29046.pdf.

Eurostat (2020). Shedding light on energy in the EU: A guided tour of energy statistics. Retrieved from: https://ec.europa.eu/eurostat/cache/infographs/energy/index.html.

Hurt, D. (2014). Egyptian general petroleum corporation (EGPC). In X. Li and M. Molina (Eds.), *Oil: A Cultural and Geographic Encyclopedia of Black Gold* (1st volume pp. 76–78). ABC-CLIO, LLC, California, USA.

Ketenci, N. (2019). Nuclear energy of Turkey in the context of the Russian Experience. In N. Ketenci and G. Bayındır Goularas (Eds.), *Turkish-Russian Relations: Prospects and Challenges* (pp. 9–16). Lexington Books, London.

Papadimitrou, J. (2008). EastMed gas pipeline flowing full of troubling questions. Deutsche Welle, 02.01.2020. Retrieved from: https://www.dw.com/en/eastmed-gas-pipeline-flowing-full-of-troubling-questions/a-51871424.

Ruble, I. (2017). European Union energy supply security: The benefits of natural gas imports from the Eastern Mediterranean. *Energy Policy*, 105, June: 341–353.

Schenk, C.J., Kirschbaum, M.A., Charpentier, R.R., Klett, T.R., Brownfield, M.E., Pitman, J.K., Cook, T.A., and Tennyson, M.E. (2010) Assessment of undiscovered oil and gas resources of the Levant Basin Province, Eastern Mediterranean: U.S. Geological Survey Fact Sheet 2010–3014, 4 p.

Sönnichsen, N. (2020). Natural gas consumption in the EU in cubic meters 1998–2018. Statista. Retrieved from: https://www.statista.com/statistics/265406/natural-gas-consumption-in-the-eu-in-cubic-meters/.

Troulis, M. (2019). The East Med pipeline project: Europe's fourth energy artery. *Civitas Gentium*, 7(2): 153–168.

Chapter 3

Energy Efficiency and Human Development in Eastern Europe's Leading Energy Supplier Countries

Ayşe Sevencan

ABSTRACT

Russia is the biggest and major energy supplier for Europe, followed by Iraq, Saudi Arabia, Norway, Kazakhstan, Nigeria, and Algeria. This chapter examines the relationship between energy efficiency, economic growth, and human development in Russia and Kazakhstan. Energy efficiency is the production per unit of energy. Compared to other developed countries, these energy suppliers have lower levels of energy efficiency. Energy efficiency not only contributes to the physical environment but also to society and the economy. Energy is a fundamental source of fulfilling basic social needs, driving economic growth, and increasing human development. However, as consumption increases, there exists a threshold where the initial positive effect of more energy consumption on human development decreases. This is mainly due to carbon emissions and environmental effects. This study takes a different approach on the energy-growth nexus and focuses on the relationship between energy efficiency and human development for energy supplier countries. The two case countries are examined in terms of energy efficiency and human development between 1990 and 2015.

Keywords: Energy, Eastern Europe, Human Development, Economic Growth

INTRODUCTION

Energy is crucial for production, but due to negative effects, such as global warming, using excessive energy in production for economic development is on a razor edge. The issue is more challenging for energy supplier countries. Russia and Kazakhstan both are energy exporters. In countries like Russia and Kazakhstan with both sufficient oil reserves and higher energy subsidization, the leading choice of input for production is energy mainly because of lower energy prices and rising domestic demand for energy. In contrast to oil-importing countries, energy-intensive production becomes a relatively cheaper way for economic growth; thus, countries like Russia and Kazakhstan are among the most energy-intensive economies.

Burning fossil fuels to generate energy release greenhouse carbon dioxide, which is a main environmental problem worldwide. Energy-intensive economies rely mostly on energy to increase production, which in turn increases carbon dioxide emissions (Lee and Chang 2008). Environmental damage is not limited to carbon dioxide emissions; it also causes damage to the health dimensions of the human capital (such as decreased life expectancy, increased mortality rates due to pollution), which is also a threat for future generations and future production. Human capital is considered as one of the main factors of production (UNDP 1990). Environmental damage to human capital jeopardizes sustainable development.

Energy efficiency is simply using less energy input to produce the same output. Oil-importing countries are mostly forced to use energy more efficiently because as the input price increases, economic theory suggests us to replace the input with lower prices. On the contrary, for oil-exporting countries, the concern on energy efficiency is forced with environmental sustainability. It is until 1990s with the United Nations Millennium Development Goals and Sustainable Development Goals, countries like Russia and Kazakhstan began to implement policies on energy efficiency.

Energy leads to economic growth at the expense of the environment, which in turn deteriorates health and thus human capital. Human capital is an essential input for sustainable development. For developing countries, the situation becomes a critical trade-off between energy and human development (Nguyen et al. 2019).

This chapter focuses on the improvements in energy efficiency in Russia and Kazakhstan and portrays the two countries' level of human development on all dimensions along with the sustainable development indicators. The chapter is organized as follows: section 2, Human Development, Sustainable Economic Growth, and Energy Consumption, section 3, Human Development and Environmental Sustainability in Russia and Kazakhstan, and section 4, Conclusion.

HUMAN DEVELOPMENT, SUSTAINABLE ECONOMIC GROWTH, AND ENERGY CONSUMPTION

Many studies in the literature aim to explain the relationship between energy consumption, human development, and sustainable economic growth.

Sustainable development covers matters such as economics, ecology, politics, technology, and society. Efficient consumption of natural resources like water, energy, and minerals gained emphasis during the last decades. Greenhouse gases, global warming, urbanization, population increase, migration, environmental degradation and destruction, industrialization, technological progress, and human development have severe negative effects on the world (Šlaus and Jacobs 2011).

In 1980, the United Nations (UN) Environment Program used the "sustainable development" phrase in the "World Conservation Strategy." In 1992, a declaration was signed in the UN held "Conference on Environment and Development" in Rio, Brazil. Best known as Agenda 21, it emphasized that all nations should take responsibility for the attainment of sustainable development in the twenty-first century. Sustainable economic growth and development may be reached if environmental sustainability is achieved through efficient energy consumption and decreasing carbon dioxide emissions that create smaller footprints for generations to come (UNDP 2012).

The UN (2015) Millennium Development Goals (MDG) aim to increase the level of human development, especially within the less developed and developing countries in particular and for all the countries, including the developed ones in general. Sustainable economic growth is supposed to ensure environmental sustainability and use energy sources accordingly. While energy consumption increases with economic and human development, new energy consumption techniques should be sought in order to decrease environmental degradation and carbon dioxide emissions.

Deichmann and Zhang's (2013) report on the Climate Action Program of Eastern and Central European countries (ECA), including both Kazakhstan and Russia, indicates that climate action in this region would benefit from rapid progress in three main areas. First, climate action would improve energy efficiency; second, local health and energy security will also improve because of clean energy systems. Finally, these economies would be more productive without increasing their carbon levels with better management of environment-friendly natural resources (Deichmann and Zhang 2013).

Not only the economic structure but also climate plays a crucial role in differences in energy efficiency rates of countries. Very cold and very hot places need more energy for heating and cooling. One other determinant of energy efficiency is the price of energy, which is expectedly lower in countries with sufficient reserves like Kazakhstan and Russia. For this reason, choosing Norway as a comparison country eliminates the climate effect and shows us the importance of economic structure, and the use of renewable sources improves energy efficiency significantly even for a country with sufficient reserves. Deichman and Zhang (2013) illustrate the case of ECA countries, in general, including Russia and Kazakhstan. They report that "if the region could match the OECD's average energy intensity, it would produce its current output using around 42% less energy, saving around 570 million tons of oil equivalent (mtoe)—or more than all of South America's energy consumption in 2009" (Deichmann and Zhang 2013, 30).

Environmental degradation is a major problem for the developing and the less developed countries that aim to achieve economic development through further production that requires more energy consumption (Cheng and Lai 1997). According to Constantini and Martini (2010), energy-saving policies do not affect economic development negatively; however, in the long run, changes in energy consumption could influence economic performance and vice versa. (Costantini and Martini 2010)

The literature on energy consumption, human development, and sustainable economic growth underlines that both economic and human development increases with efficient energy consumption. Studies mostly employ human well-being as a proxy for human development; for example, Wang et al. (2019) examine the relationship between human development and energy consumption for fifteen developing countries between 1988 and 2008. The long-run findings of energy consumption and human development analysis derive a negative relationship between these variables. These results, along with others, suggest that, although energy consumption has positive effects on human development through an increase in economic growth, thus increasing the economic well-being of individuals, in the long run, these positive effects are being offset by the possible negative effect on the health dimension of human development.

The decrease in energy consumption promotes sustainability, thereby creating more economic and human development. Jorgesson et al. (2014) examined the relationship between "energy intensity of human well-being" and economic development between 1992 and 2010 in a longitudinal analysis. They utilized a set of twelve Central and Eastern European transition countries and came to the conclusion that efficient energy usage in the so-called countries influenced human well-being and thus economic growth positively (Jorgenson, Alekseyko and Giedraitis 2014).

The sustainability of economic development is triggered by efficient energy usage, new energy services, and rising human capital. As the level of human capital increases, so does the level of economic growth and development. Alaali et al. (2015) demonstrate this fact through a panel data analysis for 130 countries for the period between 1981 and 2009. They suggest that energy consumption and human capital lead to higher economic growth for both oil-exporting and developed nations. The outcomes of the study express that whereas the developed nations are positively influenced by the education capital, the nations that export oil are negatively affected by the health capital (Alaali, Roberts, and Taylor 2015).

One other method used is the total factor energy efficiency. Qi et al. (2019) compute total factor energy efficiency (TFEE) for 60 Belt and Road Initiative (BRI) countries, including Russian and Kazakhstan, and compared them with the fifteen European Union Countries. According to their findings, average energy efficiency is significantly higher in developed EU countries. Countries with higher research and development innovation capacity, higher urbanization rate, and cleaner energy consumption have a higher capacity to catch up with advanced EU countries in terms of energy efficiency (Qi et al. 2019).

Renewable energy consumption as a percentage of the total GDP of the World Bank is one of the leading measures of green energy consumption of the relevant country. Kazakhstan and Russia both have very low shares of renewable energy consumption. A comparison with another leading exporter of energy, Norway, will be illuminating in that sense. The share of renewable energy consumption was 57.77% of the total energy consumption in 2015 in Norway. On the other hand, the share of renewable energy consumption was only 1.56 and 3.30% for the same year in Kazakhstan and Russia, respectively (World Bank 2020b).

Energy efficiency is measured with energy intensity. Energy intensity shows the ratio of energy used per unit of economic output. The higher the ratio, the higher the energy used per unit of output. Energy efficiency is the ratio between energy supply and gross domestic product measured at purchasing power parity (World Bank, 2020a).

Russia adopted the sustainable development program of the UN in 1996 and agreed on the progress of implementing sustainable development principles. UN Sustainable Development indicators are twofold. First, indicators on the quality of life such as life expectancy, health, level of knowledge and skills, employment, and degree of enforcement of rights, which are also included in the MDG. Second, a set of indicators are mainly focused on greening the economy, such as reducing resource consumption and improving energy efficiency (World Bank, 2020a).

Russia's energy efficiency policies primarily focus on the most energy-intensive sectors, such as electricity, construction of housing and communal services, manufacturing, and transport. Russia does not have a carbon tax and does not operate an emissions trading system for carbon dioxide emissions (OECD, 2018). Coal, coke, and natural gas used in agriculture, fisheries in the residential and commercial sector and in the industry are not taxed. Fuel oil and diesel are taxed in the industry and in agriculture and fisheries. In the residential and commercial sector, diesel is taxed. Other fossil fuels, as well as nonrenewable waste and biofuels, are not taxed in the economy (OECD 2019)

Russia is not close to its target as of 2015. In five years, energy intensity decreased only by 4.21% from 8.78 to 8.41 (Figure 3.1). One of the

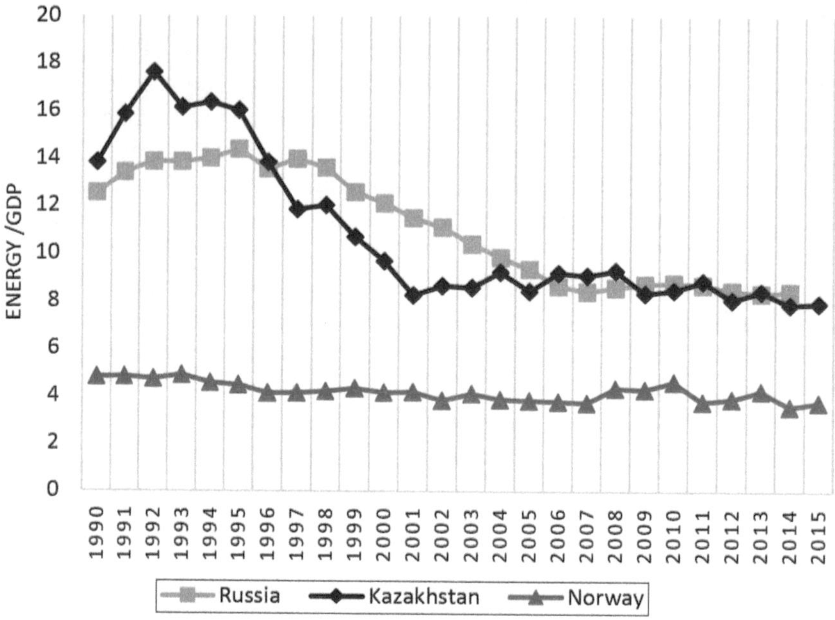

Figure 3.1 Energy intensity for the selected countries. *Source*: World Bank (2020).

possible reasons why it is not easy to decrease energy intensity is tax incentives are not promising for the firms. The country ranks fourth after China, the United States, and India, which are the major sources of greenhouse gas emissions that affect climate change, in the list of ten countries (World Bank, 2020a).

Russia tends to have relatively low average effective energy tax rates—and more energy-intensive economies. This correlation is not exclusively driven by differences in energy and carbon taxes. For instance, countries with less energy-intensive economies also tend to have less stringent regulatory mandates. There may also be structural reasons for differences in energy intensity (e.g., Ireland's knowledge-based economy, Norway's hydropower reservoirs, or Russia's oil and gas reserves), which are not necessarily the result of energy and carbon tax levels (OECD 2018).

Carbon prices are effective in terms of decreasing emissions; countries that levy higher effective carbon taxes are less carbon intensive. According to the OECD (2019), CO_2 emission intensities differ across countries for reasons that are unrelated to carbon tax levels, such as emission standards. For countries that are already less emission intensive, raising effective carbon taxes might also be politically easier. Nevertheless, the economic evidence is equally clear—carbon taxes are effective at reducing CO_2 emissions—as recently confirmed in a study that estimated the long-run effects of a broad-based carbon tax on carbon emissions from fossil fuel consumption (Sen and Vollebergh 2018).

One more crucial challenge majorly for Russia, including Kazakhstan, is that world oil production has been shifting to the United States in recent years. According to the latest report of the International Energy Agency (2019), higher oil production in the United States in recent years led the share of OPEC countries and Russia down in total oil production. This share is forecasted to be 47% in 2030, from 55% in the mid-2000s (IEA 2019). Based on the fact that both Russia and Kazakhstan rely on energy imports mostly for their economies, this report casts the importance of shifting less energy-intensive production and more efficient use of energy in these countries.

There exists a twofold relation between energy intensity and economic development. During the early stage of development, countries produce more energy-intensive products. As development continues, the need for energy diminishes. Further renewable energy in both production and consumption increases. Energy intensity increases in the first stages of development, but once the country reaches a high level of income, energy intensity in production diminishes (Ang 2004). As the level of income increases in an economy, technological advancements make it possible to use less energy to produce the same or even more output.

HUMAN DEVELOPMENT AND ENVIRONMENTAL SUSTAINABILITY IN RUSSIA AND KAZAKHSTAN HUMAN DEVELOPMENT

The HDI is a summary measure for assessing long-term progress in three basic dimensions of human development: a long and healthy life, access to knowledge, and a decent standard of living. A long and healthy life is measured by life expectancy. The knowledge level is measured by mean years of schooling among the adult population, which is the average number of years of schooling received in a life time by people aged 25 years and above, and access to learning and knowledge by expected years of schooling for children of school-entry age, which is the total number of years of schooling a child of school-entry age can expect to receive if prevailing patterns of age-specific enrolment rates stay the same throughout the child's life. Standard of living is measured by gross national income (GNI) per capita expressed in constant 2011 international dollars converted using purchasing power parity (PPP) conversion rates (UNDP 2019).

Kazakhstan's HDI value for 2018 was 0.817—which put the country in the very high human development category—positioning it at 50 out of 189 countries and territories. The rank is shared with Belarus. Between 1990 and 2018, Kazakhstan's life expectancy at birth increased by 6.5 years (from 66.8 to 73.2 years), mean years of schooling increased by 3.7 years (from 8.1 to 11.8 years), and expected years of schooling increased by 2.9 years (from 12.4 to 15.3). Kazakhstan's GNI per capita increased by about 61.8% between 1990 and 2018 (from 13.703 USD to 22.168 USD) (World Bank 2020c).

Kazakhstan's 2018 HDI of 0.817 is below the average of 0.892 for countries in the very high human development group and above the average of 0.779 for countries in Europe and Central Asia. From Europe and Central Asia, countries which were close to Kazakhstan in 2018 HDI rank and to some extent in population size are Russian Federation and Ukraine, which have HDIs ranked 49 and 88, respectively (UNDP 2019) (World Bank 2020c).

Russian Federation's HDI value for 2018 was 0.824—which put the country in the very high human development category—positioning it at 49 out of 189 countries and territories. Between 1990 and 2018, the Russian Federation's HDI value increased from 0.734 to 0.824, an increase of 12.3%. Between 1990 and 2018, the Russian Federation's life expectancy at birth increased by 4.3 years, mean years of schooling increased by 2.8 years, and expected years of schooling increased by 2.7 years. Russian Federation's GNI per capita increased from 20.898 USD to 25.036 USD, by about 19.8% between 1990 and 2018 (UNDP 2019).

ENVIRONMENTAL SUSTAINABILITY

Burning natural gas leads to carbon dioxide, and it is one of the leading sources of environmental problems. Using energy efficiently could save most of the oil to be a dangerous waste. IEA (2011) estimates that Russia could have saved 200 million tons of oil or 30% of total consumption if it had an energy efficiency rate close to countries like Norway. However, even with these savings, Russia and Kazakhstan would have a higher energy consumption than the OECD average. The two main reasons are energy-intensive industries and climate (IEA 2011). Air pollution due to power generation has effects on the health of the public. According to Deichman and Zhang (2013), this cost is around $20 billion in ECA each year.

Kazakhstan's energy sector is mostly based on coal. However, the country is focused on increasing the share of renewable sources and expanding the gas pipeline network to reduce dependence on coal and LPG. Kazakhstan is also part of the EU4 energy policy project, an initiative focused on evidence-based policymaking for the energy sector (IEA 2019). The Green Economy program in Kazakhstan proposes green economic growth and puts a special emphasis on urbanization, to increase from 56 to 70% (UNDP 2019).

The environmental sustainability indicators present the levels of or changes in energy consumption, carbon dioxide emissions, forest area, freshwater withdrawals, and natural resource depletion. Environmental threat indicators are mortality rates attributed to household and ambient air pollution, and to unsafe water, sanitation and hygiene services, percentage of land that is degraded, and the International Union for Conservation of Nature Red List Index value, which measures the change in aggregate extinction risk across groups of species (UNDP 2019).

In terms of environmental sustainability, currently, both countries do perform well. In 2015, the share of renewable energy consumption as a percentage of total energy consumption was 3.3% in Russia and was only 1.6% in Kazakhstan, and they both ranked among the bottom third of the countries in this category (World Bank 2020). Mortality rates attributed to air pollution[1] is 49 and 63 in 100,000 people in Russia and Kazakhstan, respectively, placing both countries in the middle third of 189 countries (World Bank 2020b).

The Energy Efficiency Project of the World Bank for the Republic of Kazakhstan, which was approved in May 2013, aims to improve energy efficiency and endure sustainable energy financing. The project involves both investment and technical assistance. The first part is financing eligible subprojects to support a reduction in energy use of public buildings such as schools, kindergartens, clinics/hospitals, and street lighting. The second part concerns technical assistance (TA) to help ensure effective project implementation. The total project cost is US$ 23.06 million, and the closing date of the Project is December 29, 2020 (Kohli 2020).

CONCLUSION

This study examines the trends in energy efficiency and human development in Russia and Kazakhstan for the 1990 and 2015 period. In the past three decades, environmental consciousness has increased worldwide. Both countries are on the path to increase energy efficiency. The dilemma for oil-exporting countries is that in order to promote economic growth, these countries with lower energy prices and subsidies become more and more energy intensive. In the long run, however, environmental externalities would offset the short-run benefits. Especially for health outcomes, these countries will face the challenge of high health costs, lower employment levels, and lower quality human capital, which are also crucial for sustainable economic development. Both countries should focus on policies to increase energy efficiency and shift to renewable sources of energy. Energy-related policies should be designed to be tax-efficient on the producer side of the economy. Tax incentives could shift production to more efficient or renewable sources via subsidies for renewables and higher taxes for pollutants.

NOTE

1. Mortality rate attributed to household and ambient air pollution: Age-standardized mortality rate resulting from exposure to ambient (outdoor) air pollution and household (indoor) air pollution from solid fuel use for cooking, expressed per 100,000 population. Ambient air pollution results in emissions from industrial activity, households, cars, and trucks (World Bank 2020b).

REFERENCES

Alaali, F., J. Roberts, and K. Taylor. 2015. "The effect of energy consumption and human capital on economic growth: An exploration of oil exporting and developed countries." *Sheffield Economic Research Paper*, ISSN 1749-8368.

Ang, Beng, W. 2004. "Decomposition analysis for policymaking in energy: which is the preferred method?" *Energy Policy* 32 (9): 1131–1139.

Cheng, Benjamin S., and Tin Wei Lai. 1997. "An investigation of co-integration and causality between energy consumption and economic activity in Taiwan." *Energy Economics* 19 (4): 435–444.

Costantini, Valeria, and Chiara Martini. 2010. "The causality between energy consumption and economic growth: A multi-sectoral analysis using non-stationary cointegrated panel data." *Energy Economics* 32 (3): 591–603.

Damette, Olivier, and Majda Seghir. 2013. "Energy as a driver of growth in oil exporting countries?" *Energy Economics* 37 (C): 193–199.

Deichmann, Uwe, and Fan Zhang. 2013. *Growing Green: The Economic Benefits of Climate Action.* Eastern Europe and Central Asia Reports, Washington, DC: World Bank.

IEA. 2011. "World Energy Outlook 2011." Pari: IEA.

IEA. 2019. *World Energy Outlook.* Paris: IEA.

Jorgenson, Andrew K., Alina Alekseyko, and Vincentas Giedraitis. 2014. "Energy consumption, human well-being and economic development in central and eastern Europe: A cautionary tale of sustainability." *Energy Policy* 66 (4): 419–427.

Kohli, Sandeep. 2020. *Disclosable Version of the ISR—Kazakhstan Energy Efficiency Project - P130013.* Washington, DC: World Bank Group.

Lee, Chien-Chiang, and Chun-Ping, Chang. 2008. "Energy consumption and economic growth in Asian economies: A more comprehensive analysis using panel data." *Resource and Energy Economics* 30 (1): 50–65.

Matraeva, Lilia, Petr Solodukha, Sergey Erokhin, and Maria Babenko. 2019. "Improvement of Russian energy efficiency strategy within the framework of "green economy" concept (based on the analysis of experience of foreign countries)." *Energy Policy* 125: 478–486.

Nguyen, Van Tran, Van Tran Quyet, Linh, Hong Dinh Linh Thi Thuy Do, and Thi Thu Do Ha. 2019. "Trade off between environment, energy consumption and human development: Do levels of economic development matter?" *Energy* Volume 173: 483–493, ISSN 0360-5442.

OECD. 2018. *Effective Carbon Rates 2018: Pricing Carbon Emissions through Taxes and Emissions Trading*. Paris: OECD Publishing.

OECD. 2019. *Taxing Energy Use 2019: Using Taxes for Climate Action*. Paris: OECD Publishing.

Qi, Shaozhou, Huarong Penga, Xiaoling Zhang, and Xiujie Tan. 2019. "Is energy efficiency of Belt and Road Initiative countries catching up or falling behind? Evidence from a panel quantile regression approach." *Applied Energy* 253: 113581.

Sen, Suphi, and Herman Vollebergh. 2018. "The effectiveness of taxing the carbon content of energy consumption." *Journal of Environmental Economics and Management* 92: 74–99.

Šlaus, Ivo, and Garry Jacobs. 2011. "Human Capital and Sustainability." *Sustainability* 3 (1): 97–154.

UNDP. 1990. *Human development report*. Report for the United Nations Development Program, New York: Oxford University Press.

UNDP. 2012. "Report on Implementing The Principles of Sustainable Development in The Russian Federation. Russian Outlook on the New Paradigm for Sustainable Development. Preparing For 'RIO + 20'." *Sustainable Development UN*. https://sustainabledevelopment.un.org/content/documents/1043natrepeng.pdf.

UNDP. 2019a. "Human Development Report 2019: Beyond Income, Beyond Averages, Beyond Today—Inequalities in Human Development in the 21st Century." United Nations, New York.

UNDP. 2019b. *Urbanization as an Accelerator of Inclusive and Sustainable Development*. 2019 Kazakhstan Human Development Report, UNDP.

Wang, Xingyu, Heran Zheng, Zhenyu Wang, Yuli Shan, Jing Meng, Xi Liang, Kuishuang Feng, and Dabo Guan. 2019. "Kazakhstan's CO_2 emissions in the post-Kyoto Protocol era: Production and consumption based analysis." *Journal of Environmental Management* 249: 109393, https://doi.org/10.1016/j.jenvman.2019.109393.

World Bank. 2020a. "Sustainable Energy for All." *World Bank Data*. 4 10. Accessed August 20, 2020. https://datacatalog.worldbank.org/dataset/sustainable-energy-all.

World Bank. 2020b. *World Bank Data*. 07 17. https://data.worldbank.org/indicator/EG.FEC.RNEW.ZS?locations=KZ-RU-NO.

World Bank. 2020c. "Kazahstan Economic Update." *Sustaining Growth Momentum*. http://documents.worldbank.org/curated/en/738861576757431754/Kazakhstan-Economic-Update-Sustaining-Growth-Momentum.

Chapter 4

Search for Gaining Economic and Political Power without Any Resources

Levent Çağrı Uslu

ABSTRACT

Throughout the modern era, countries with abundant energy resources have created an economic benefit from these resources. Yet, recently, having abundant energy also enabled countries to also gain political power. Russia, for instance, is a good example of such countries. On the contrary, without having any energy resources (excluding some limited oil extraction from Raman Mountain, Batman), Turkey started to gain both economic and political power by just acting as a hub between the largest energy suppliers and demanders. More specifically, oil and natural gas extracted from the Caspian Sea and the Middle East are carried to the European market via the pipelines passing through Turkey. More recently, the discovery of abundant natural gas in the Eastern Mediterranean further increased the importance of Turkey in "Energy Game" of Europe and the Middle East. Turkey has been signing agreements and constructing the pipeline infrastructure to carry Caspian and the Middle East originated energy to the European market. On the contrary, Europe desperately needs the energy imported from these regions not just only to satisfy market demand but also to achieve diversity in energy sources and break the burden of being stuck to one particular source. This chapter aims to take a snapshot of the economic and political importance of current and planned pipelines (oil and natural gas) passing through Turkey. It will also focus on current developments at the Eastern Mediterranean from an economical and political perspective.

Keywords: Energy, Middle East, Turkey, Political Power, Economic Gain

INTRODUCTION

The history of natural gas as an energy source dates back to 1959 with the discovery of the Groningen field in the Netherlands. Later, the British discovered reserves in the UK sector of the North Sea. Both reserves were used to satisfy domestic energy demand. However, the game changed after Norwegians, with low domestic energy demand, discovering huge gas supplies and started exporting them to the United Kingdom and continental Europe. Starting from the late 1940s, Russia was exporting Natural Gas to Poland, yet in very small quantities. After discovering super-giant gas fields of Medvezhe, Urengoy, and Yamburg, during the 1970s and 1980s, large-diameter pipelines were laid between Ukraine and these super-giant gas fields, which then needed some minor extensions to transport the Russian gas to the European market. The third major natural gas suppliers are the African countries, namely Algeria and Nigeria. The first gas started to flow from Tunisia to Italy in late 1983. Later, in 1996, a second pipeline transporting North African natural gas to the European market passing through Algeria, Morocco, and Spain started operating (Craig, Gerali, MacAulay, & Sorkhabi, 2018). All these developments formed a new industry, which accounts for almost 20% of energy demand in Europe by the late twentieth century and expected to account for 30% by 2030.

The search for different suppliers arises from two facts: (a) to satisfy the increasing gas demand and (b) to ensure energy security. From the first point, it may be argued that Russia itself may supply the entire gas that Europe needs. However, regarding the second fact, relying on just one energy supplier, to a certain extent, implies an increase in political power for the supplier. The import dependency of natural gas in 2020 is projected to be 65 and 72% to 73% by 2030. Due to this high import dependency on natural gas, in 2008, the directorate general for Energy and Transport of the European Commission prepared a report on EU gas security and interconnectivity of natural gas pipelines. This report constituted the backbone of EU's Strategy for Trans-European Energy Networks and EU Security of Gas Supply Regulation. The stability of the EU's energy supply may be threatened if a high proportion of imports are concentrated among relatively few external partners (European Commission, 2016).

The Union faced a major gas supply interruption in the winters of 2008 and 2009 due to political problems between Russia and Ukraine. The purpose of the strategy is to prevent such interruptions in the natural gas supply. Thus, diversification in natural gas supply is inevitable in the context of European energy policies. From this point of view, natural gas supply from a fourth region is in accordance with the master strategy of the Union. Therefore, natural gas supply from the Caspian, Iran, and Arab World is an important element in energy security.

In addition to the above-mentioned natural gas fields, a new gas reserve has been recently discovered in the Eastern Mediterranean (East Med Gas) that may also be transported to the European market through Turkey. The term "East Med Gas" refers to an offshore gas field off the southern coast of the natural gas fields of Cyprus. The field is shared by two countries, Cyprus (Aphrodite Gas Field) and Israel (Tamar and Leviathan gas fields). Aphrodite gas field (more specifically Block 12 located 34 km west of Israel's Leviathan gas field) has an estimated average of 200 billion cubic meters of natural gas. The Israeli Leviathan gas field has an estimated average of 450 billion cubic meters, whereas the Tamar gas field has an estimated 223 billion cubic meters of natural gas. The East Med Gas field is estimated to cover 4% or 10 billion cubic meters of European Gas demand (Pepple & Baker, 2020).

These facts give Turkey an opportunity to act as a hub between some of the largest natural gas reserves and the European market since it rests between these two actors of the natural gas market. It has a geopolitical advantage to act as a hub between the Caspian, Middle East, and Iranian and the European market. Not only these countries but also Russian gas may be transported via pipelines passing through Anatolia.

FACTS AND FIGURES IN THE EUROPEAN NATURAL GAS MARKET

The total natural gas consumption in Europe is close to 500 billion cubic meters per year. As of the first quarter of 2019 (Figure 4.1), the most important natural gas supplier is Russia (40%) followed by Norway (29%), Algeria (11%), Qatar (7.2%), and Nigeria (4.4%). Other countries constitute roughly 8% of total gas supplies (Eurostat). The major pipelines may be categorized into three: (a) the North Sea, (b) Russia, and (c) Africa. Pipelines transferring gas from the North Sea (Europipe I, II, Nogat, Franpipe, Zeepipe, etc.) This first group of supply referred to as indigenous supply. These pipelines have an annual gas discharge capacity of approximately 150 billion cubic meters. The second group of pipelines is the one that links Russian gas fields to Europe (Nordstream I, Northern Lights, Brotherhood, Soyuz, Urgenoy-Pomary-Uzhgorod, Bluestream, Gaswest). The total discharge capacity of pipelines stretching from Russian super-giant gas fields to the European market reaches approximately 250 billion cubic meters. Moreover, the planned pipelines account for some 100 billion cubic meters of discharge capacity. Finally, the African, as well as Nigerian, natural gas is supplied to the European market by four pipelines (Greenstream, MEG, Medgas, Trans-Mediterranean) with

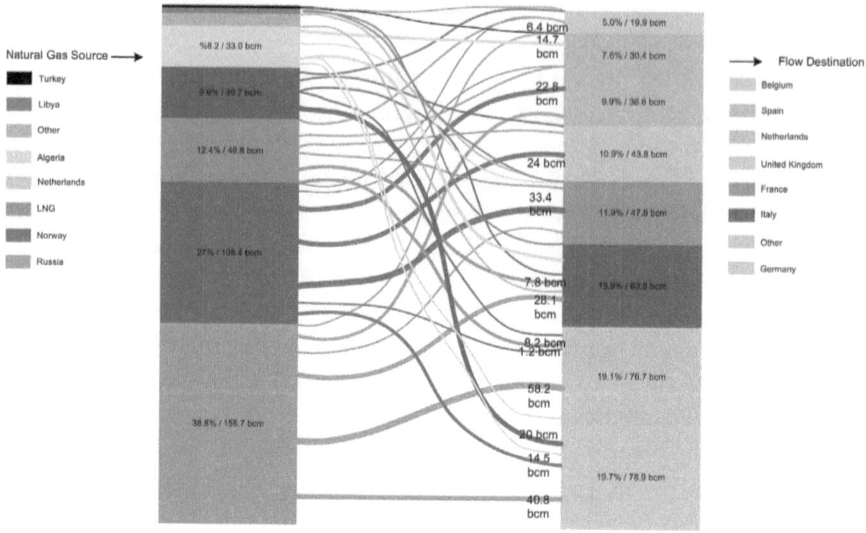

Figure 4.1 European natural gas flows, bcm. *Source*: Energy Insights EU Pipe Flow; ALSI; AGSI.

a total annual discharge capacity of 60 billion cubic meters of natural gas. A planned fifth pipeline (Galsi) has a discharge capacity of 10 billion cubic meters. Figures reveal that the total discharge capacity of the pipelines from Africa to the European market is only slightly higher than NordStream I (www.wikipedia.com, Quarterly Report on European Gas Markets 2020).

Ritter (2010) argues that more than 80% of global natural gas reserves are within reach of pipelines, which enables the EU to virtually secure the supply. Moreover, liquefied natural gas (LNG) regasification terminals have the potential to survive European economies. Thus, the EU will not run out of natural gas in the foreseeable future. Yet it will become even more important for the old continent to evaluate the risks of the high import dependency in the natural gas market.

From this point of view, it is important for the EU to have a fourth and (or even fifth) link to natural gas–supplying regions. Southern Gas Corridor (SGC) is, therefore, inevitable for the European market. SGC is one of the most complex projects of the world, stretching over 3,500 km, passing through six countries (Azerbaijan, Georgia, Turkey, Greece, Albania, and Italy). The corridor may be separated into three subprojects: (a) South Caucasus Pipeline (SCPX) from Azerbaijan to Georgia; (b) Trans Anatolian Pipeline (TANAP), Turkey; and (c) Trans Adriatic Pipeline (TAP) passing through Greece, Albania, and Italy. The project initially aims to carry Caspian Natural Gas (namely, The Shah Deniz reservoir of Azerbaijan) to the European market. The project also proposes some future opportunities (NsEnergyBusiness).

According to the European Commission's "Second Strategic Energy Review" (2008), in addition to above-mentioned countries, the EU identified Turkmenistan, Kazakhstan, Iraq, Mashreq[1] countries, and if conditions hold, Uzbekistan and Iran as partner countries. The region comprised of above-mentioned countries has a total natural gas reserve of 90 trillion cubic meters (44% of global proven reserves) of natural gas. If we exclude those reserves that are unfeasible for the European market to import via pipelines, it is evident that these countries have more than 55% of natural gas feasible for the European market (Second Strategic Energy Review an EU Energy Security and Solidarity Action Plan, 2008).

A similar set of relationships are now emerging further south in the Eastern Mediterranean, where Israel, Cyprus, and Egypt are forming strategic triangles of their own, which exclude Turkey. One of the principal reasons behind the political alignment between these three countries to explore natural gas pipeline projects is political tensions with Ankara. Israel–Turkey relations collapsed in summer 2010 when Israeli commandos launched a deadly raid on a Turkish ship trying to deliver humanitarian aid to Gaza. Though Turkey and Israel finally restored diplomatic relations at the end of 2016, relations soured again in late 2017, when President Donald Trump announced the US Embassy move from Tel Aviv to Jerusalem, which resulted in Turkish President Recep Tayyip Erdoğan lashing out against Israel. Cyprus and Turkey, meanwhile, have no diplomatic relations, as Ankara does not recognize the existence of the Greek Cypriot-led Republic of Cyprus. Finally, Egypt–Turkey relations have been tensed since the then General Abdel Fattah al-Sisi overthrew the Muslim Brotherhood-led government of Mohammed Morsi in summer 2013.

DECOMPOSING THE EASTMED PROBLEM

The EastMed natural gas problem may be decomposed into two: (a) who owns the gas and (b) how will the gas be transported to the European market? However, these two problems are not mutually exclusive problems but instead somehow complex problems. Solving one issue requires a solution to the other issue.

The first problem, who owns the gas, has deeper roots: the problem of delimiting the territorial sea and exclusive economic zone (EEZ) between Turkey and Greece—ongoing, unsolved issue between these two bordering countries. The concept of territorial sea emerged in the 1940s. In particular, in the Aegean Sea, the emergence of problems related to restricted areas of the territorial sea between Turkey and Greece have found the beginning of the 1970s. Since then, the issue remains unsolved. In principle, Greece aims to increase its territorial sea up to the maximum distance that was permitted by the United Nations Convention on the Law of the Sea. On the contrary, Turkey claims that, due to the closeness of Greek islands to mainland Turkey, the continental shelf should be as much as 6 miles. The Convention of Continental Shelf argues that disputes between countries should be solved by bilateral agreements, yet there is none between Turkey and Greece. Even if the continental shelf remained at 6 miles, 40% of Aegean Sea belongs to Greece, an increase in the continental shelf to 12 miles increases this percentage to 71, and only less than 10% falls within the Turkish continental shelf. This imbalance caused by Greek islands precludes a possible solution.

A problem different from the territorial sea, but firmly linked to it, is the unsolved issue of EEZ[2] (Figure 4.2). In November 2019, Turkey and Libya signed a deal, which created an EEZ from the southern Turkish coast to Libya's north-east coast (Cohen, 2020). Egypt opposed the deal and argued that it was illegal. Greece argued that such a deal was impossible due to the existence of the Greek island of Crete, midway between the two countries. Response from Greece and Egypt came on August 6, 2020. Two countries created and EEZ, but this time, Turkey argues that the deal falls on its continental shelf (Aljazeera, 2020). As a result, undiscovered natural gas between Crete and Cyprus is claimed by four countries, but in principle by Turkey and Greece.

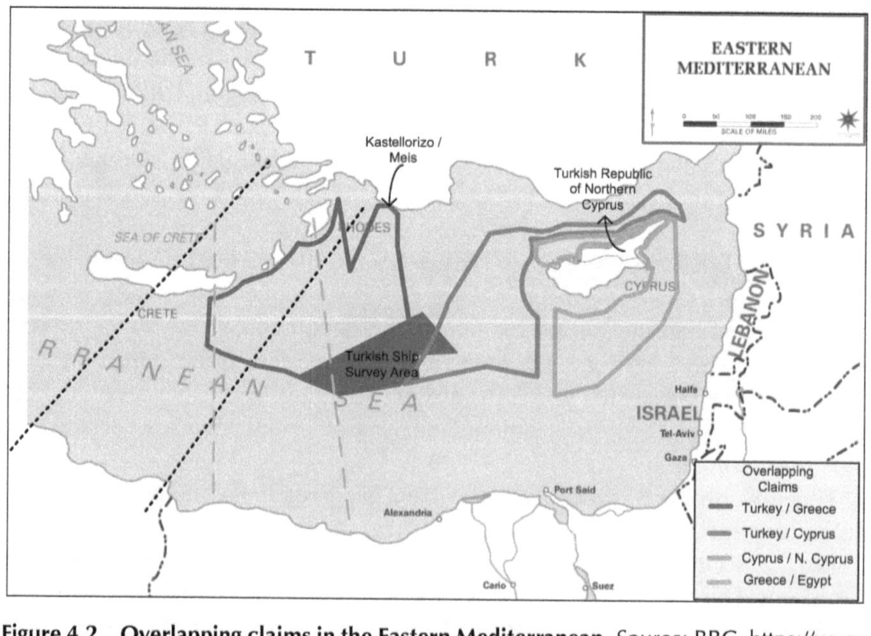

Figure 4.2 Overlapping claims in the Eastern Mediterranean. *Source*: BBC, https://www.bbc.com/news/world-europe-53906360.

The second problem (i.e., how will the gas be transported to the European market), unfortunately, is also related to the above-mentioned first problem. On January 2, 2020, a gas pipeline deal was signed by Cyprus, Greece, and Israel to transfer gas extracted from the Aphrodite Gas Field of Greece and the Tamar and Leviathan gas fields of Israel. The proposed pipeline is seen as one option of tapping EastMed gas supplies for the EU alongside shipping it to the EU by tankers in the form of LNG. Although LNG is an option to transfer natural gas, high transportation costs make it unfeasible. The proposed 1,900 km subsea pipeline starts from the gas fields, then to Cyprus, Crete, mainland Greece, and finally reaches Italy and is planned to discharge between 9 and 12 billion cubic meters of natural gas to the European Market (Staff, 2018). Yet there are two problems associated with the proposed EastMed pipeline: (a) it passes through EEZ deal between Libya and Turkey and (b) Turkey argues that Turkey is the most commercially feasible and secure route for the utilization of natural resources in the Eastern Mediterranean and their transfer to the consumer markets in Europe, including Turkey (Michalopoulos, 2020).

Although Turkey's opposition to the project, Greece and Israel aim to reach a final investment decision by 2022 and complete it by 2025. The pact between Turkey and Libya could present a barrier to the proposed pipeline, which would have to cross the planned Turkey–Libya economic zone.

TREATS AND OPPORTUNITIES

Geopolitical thinkers enjoy drawing some potential strategic lines on maps. Big infrastructure projects, such as the one under consideration, are seen as catalysts of new geopolitical cooperation. However, the truth, in most cases, is different from what these super-optimistic thinkers. The preliminary condition that these mega infrastructure projects need to create geopolitical cooperation is the existence of common goals (i.e., Azerbaijan, Georgia and Turkey), which is lacking in the focus of this study. Once this occurs, these projects can work on behalf of new vectors of strategic collaboration. Otherwise, it is evident that a clash of interests may lead to political crisis and even to war (Bryza, 2018).

A set of relationships that geopolitical thinkers argue emerged in the Eastern Mediterranean, formed by Israel, Cyprus, Greece, and Egypt, excluding Turkey. The exclusion of Turkey has backgrounding reasons. With Greece (and Cyprus) above-mentioned reason; with Israel, the Mavi Marmara incident in 2010 and the declaration of Jerusalem as capital in 2017; and finally with Egypt, support to Mohammed Morsi during and after the military takeover led by General Abdel Fattah al-Sisi (Tsakiris, Ulgen, & Han, 2018).

As a matter of fact, still one cannot prevent asking that crucial question: is it still possible to establish geopolitical cooperation? Will this one-decade old developments in the region create an opportunity to basically establish stronger political and economic links between Turkey, Greece, and Israel? Will Turkey and Greece use this opportunity to solve their never-ending problems?

TURKEY–GREECE RELATIONS

This is the most complex set of relations in the EastMed gas puzzle. The two neighboring countries engaged in a war four times in their history and experienced some heat-ups during recent decades. Yet this latest controversy related to gas reserves, territorial seas, and EEZ have increased fears that tension between these two countries may further increase. At the beginning of 2017, the messages from politicians (i.e., former minister of Energy of Turkey Berat Albayrak, minister of Foreign Affairs of Turkey Mevlüt Çavuşoğlu, former Greek prime minister Alexis Tsipras) from both countries where giving softer speeches yet giving strong messages to their opponents and the rest of the world, namely, to the European Union and to the United States. It was maybe this period that the EastMed natural gas issue may have given impetus to advanced cooperation between these two countries.

However, since then, steps taken by both countries muff this chance. The agreement between Israel, Cyprus, and Greece, the deal of EEZ between Turkey and Libya, the actions of Fatih, Kanuni, and Yavuz drilling ships in addition to Oruç Reis, issuing Navtex first in the East Mediterranean and recently in the Aegean Sea have increased the tension between these two countries.

Following Germany's intervention, in early September 2020, Turkey "paused" offshore surveys near the Greek islands, south of Kastellorizo, in order to enable dialogue with Greece to address the disputes between the two countries (Geropoulos, 2020).

Apart from this increase in tension between Turkey and Greece, there are still some prudent politicians in both countries who argue that the discovery of giant natural gas fields in the Eastern Mediterranean still creates an opportunity for these two countries to strongly bound. Efklidis Tsakalotos, minister of Economy during the former Syriza government, argues that "it is surely Greece's right to establish new deals with Eastern Mediterranean countries, but this should not be done by leaving Turkey apart. Moreover, a possible solution within EU legislation will help Turkey to get closer to become a full member of the EU."

Former Greek foreign minister, Nikos Kocyas, argued that "If one argues that whatever there is in Mediterranean belongs to Greece and only Greece is nothing but just a part of the problem" (Takvim, 2020).

On the other hand, Mevlüt Çavuşoğlu, current minister of Foreign Affairs, argued in an article in Kethimerini that "the logic of 'permanent neighbor' naturally entails mutual respect for each other's rights. . . . Such mutual respect in turn should be manifest in a sense of obligation to solve all pending issues or outstanding conflicts through peaceful means and dialogue. In such a spirit, neighbors do not seek escalation, but seek direct diplomacy and dialogue in good faith and with an aim for genuine dispute resolution" (Çavuşoğlu, 2020).

One can find numerous examples. However, unfortunately, both countries are missing the opportunity of establishing closer relations and solving never-ending disputes with the help of energy policies in the Eastern Mediterranean.

TURKEY–ISRAEL RELATIONS

Given their geopolitical importance on the region, Israel and Turkey have had the opportunity to establish long-lasting regional cooperation. Yet the recent developments in relations between these two countries are not promising. The one but a highly essential fact in the state of affairs is the Palestinian–Israeli relations. Turkey's relations with Israel also form an important part of Turkey's domestic politics. In this respect, "the ebb and flow of relations can be connected to the political attitudes and behaviors of social forces in Turkey's domestic political space" (Balcı & Kardaş, 2012). Incidents, in chronological order like the Operation Cast Lead in Gaza, the debate between Shimon Peres and then prime minister Recep Tayyip Erdoğan, the Israeli attack on Mavi Marmara, and finally the declaration of Jerusalem as the capital have halted the political relations between Israel and Turkey. Recently, the Israeli side restrains itself in diplomatic relations. According to some, the main reason behind this attitude of Israel is to overcome a possible pressure to get Israel's new-found gas reserves to European markets through a pipeline from Israel's giant Leviathan field to either the Turkish port of Ceyhan or directly combining it to TANAP. By doing so, Turkey is aiming to establish a Special Energy Industry zone which in turn will generate political power. It could be said that overall Turkish attitudes toward the issue of East Med Gas transportation routes have been, and largely still are, predicated on the indispensability of the Turkish route. Thus, long-term reconciliation of political relations between these two countries desperately needs patience, persistence, and prudence, which is not an easy task under current circumstances.

CONCLUSION

The natural gas demand in the European Union is largely satisfied by imports, basically from the Russian Federation. Yet the Union is searching for different natural gas supplies. The search for different suppliers arises from two facts: (a) to satisfy the increasing gas demand and (b) to ensure energy security. This search also turns the Unions attention to eastern gas fields such as Shah Sea, Qatar, and even Kazakhstan.

The recently discovered Aphrodite gas field of Cyprus and Leviathan gas field of Israel are good options for the European Union. The potential of discovering natural gas fields has triggered the drilling activities in the Eastern Mediterranean. However, dominant countries acting in the Eastern Mediterranean, namely Israel, Greece, and Turkey, have long-lasting disputes. Moreover, the decades-long territorial sea dispute between Turkey and Greece threatens peaceful, collaborative solutions to extracting and marketing the natural gas that will most probably be extracted in the region. Since the dispute between Turkey and Israel is more like a diplomatic issue and does not involve any territorial facts, and since throughout history, these two countries had relatively good relations, it proposes a higher potential be solved.

Recent developments in the region, such as the EEZ deal between Turkey and Libya, and the agreement between Israel, Egypt, and Greece, in addition to military actions of France, Greece, and Turkey, further deepen the problem rather than using this potential giant infrastructure investment as an opportunity to establish strong relations and solving the regional issues. Besides these developments, as of September 2020, Turkey suspended its drilling activities and gave a chance to Germany-led attempt to a peaceful solution to the issue. This, hopefully, will start a new era, which is characterized by solutions to never-ending disputes.

NOTES

1. Bahrain, Sudan, Saudi Arabia, Qatar, Yemen, Oman, Kuwait, the United Arab Emirates, Jordan, Lebanon, Syria, and Palestine.
2. Both Exclusive Economic Zone and Continental Shelf concepts address 200 nautical miles from the coast line yet their judicial meanings are completely different. For the sake of simplicity, we will stick to Exclusive Economic Zone concept.

REFERENCES

Aljazeera. (2020). Turkey denounces maritime deal between Greece, Egypt. Aljazeera. Retrieved from https://www.aljazeera.com/news/2020/08/turkey-denounces-maritime-deal-greece-egypt-200807065300640.html.

Balcı, A., & Kardaş, T. (2012). The changing dynamics of Turkey's relations with Israel: An analysis of 'Securitization'. *Insight Turkey*, 14, 99–120.

Bryza, M. J. (2018). East Med Energy: Restoring Squandered Opportunities. Retrieved from http://turkishpolicy.com/article/935/east-med-energy-restoring-squandered-opportunities.

Çavuşoğlu, M. (2020). "Our Preference in Eastern Mediterranean is Diplomacy without Preconditions. Retrieved from http://www.mfa.gov.tr/sayin-bakanimizin-kathimerini-makalesi.en.mfa.

Cohen, A. (2020). Turkey-Libya Maritime Deal Upsets Mediterranean Energy Plan. Forbes. Retrieved from https://www.forbes.com/sites/arielcohen/2020/01/08/turkey-libya-maritime-deal-upsets-mediterranean-energy-plan/#6bc381a26bee.

Craig, J., Gerali, F., MacAulay, F., & Sorkhabi, R. (2018). The history of the European oil and gas industry (1600s–2000s). *Geological Society Publications,* Special Publications, 1–24. doi: https://doi.org/10.1144/SP465.23.

European Commission (2016). European Commission Security of Gas Supply Regulation Report. European Commission, Brussels. Retrieved from https://ec.europa.eu/commission/presscorner/detail/sv/MEMO_16_308.

Geropoulos, K. (2020). Greece-Egypt EEZ deal doesn't sit easy with Turkey. Retrieved from https://www.neweurope.eu/article/greece-egypt-eez-deal-doesnt-sit-easy-with-turkey/.

Michalopoulos, S. (2020). EU welcomes EastMed gas pipe deal as 'one option' to strengthen energy security. Euractiv. Retrieved from https://www.euractiv.com/section/energy/news/eu-welcomes-eastmed-deal-but-highlights-further-cost-benefit-analysis/.

NsEnergyBusiness. (n.d.). Shah Deniz Gas Field Development. Retrieved from https://www.nsenergybusiness.com/projects/shah-deniz-gas-field-development/.

Pepple, S., & Baker, M. (2020). Border Disputes and Gas Fields in The Eastern Mediterranean. Foreign Affairs. Retrieved from https://www.foreignaffairs.com/border-disputes-and-gas-fields-eastern-mediterranean.

European Commission (2020). Quarterly Report on European Gas Markets. European Commission, Brussels. Retrieved from https://ec.europa.eu/energy/sites/ener/files/quarterly_report_on_european_gas_markets_q1_2020.pdf.

Ritter, A. (2010). The EU's Gas Security of Supply: Risk Analysis and Management. College of Europe Department of ECU International Relations and Diplomacy Studies. Retrieved from https://www.coleurope.eu/system/files_force/research-paper/edp_10_2011_ritter.pdf?download=1.

Commission of the Europ COMMUNITIES (2008). Second Strategic Energy Review an EU Energy Security and Solidarity Action Plan. Retrieved from https://eur-lex.europa.eu/LexUriServ/LexUriServ.do?uri=COM:2008:0781:FIN:EN:PDF.

Staff, T. (2018). Israel, Cyprus, and Greece push East Med gas pipeline to Europe. The Times of Israel. Retrieved from Israel, Cyprus, and Greece push East Med gas pipeline to Europe.

Takvim. (2020). Yunanistan'ın akil insanları savaş istemiyor! https://www.takvim.com.tr/guncel/2020/09/06/yunanistanin-akil-insanlari-savas-istemiyor

Tsakiris, T., Ulgen, S., & Han, A. K. (2018). Gas Developments in the Eastern Mediterranean: Trigger or Obstacle for EUTurkey Cooperation? FEUTURE. Retrieved from file:///C:/Users/tyg/Downloads/FEUTURE_EastMed_May2018.pdf.

Chapter 5

Energy as a Complicating Factor

Conflict in the Eastern Mediterranean and the New Challenges in Cyprus Question

Gizem Alioğlu Çakmak and Melih Güner

ABSTRACT

The geostrategic significance of the Eastern Mediterranean region increased dramatically as a result of discoveries of new energy resources. The enhanced drilling and exploration activities of several countries led to the emergence of new crises in the region. All the parties involved have their own competing claims over maritime borders, exclusive economic zones (EEZs) and gas, and oil deposits.

The energy question in the East Mediterranean region also started to function as a complicating factor in the traditional Cyprus question. When Turkey started its maritime operations in the region, the EU sided by Greece and the Greek Cypriot Government announced to take measures against Turkey. The Greek Cypriot government (the RoC government) accuses Turkey of violating its economic zones and rights in the region. Turkey, on the other hand, argues that its operations take place where Turkish Cypriots have rights and on its continental shelf. The Cyprus issue has always been a major concern in Turkish–Greek relations. Thus, the increased tension in the region and the complication of the Cyprus dispute have had a significant impact on the bilateral relations of Turkey and Greece.

The main purpose of this chapter is to analyze the impact of the energy crisis in the Eastern Mediterranean Region on the bilateral relations of Turkey and Greece. While doing so, the official statements of Turkish and Greek Foreign Ministries will be scrutinized.

Keywords: Turkish - Greek Relations, Turkish Cypriots, Greek Cypriot Government, Eastern Mediterranean

ENERGY AND THE EASTERN MEDITERRANEAN

The Eastern Mediterranean, historically, has always been a very important region. Owing to its strategic location and natural resources, this region causes power struggles between regional powers. For decades, Eastern Mediterranean maritime border conflicts have been a local issue, limited to sovereignty claims and counterclaims among Cyprus, Greece, and Turkey[1]. However, the emergence of new energy resources and enhanced drilling activities have turned the East Med into a key strategic region of conflict and competition.

Israel started to search for hydrocarbon zones in the Eastern Mediterranean in 1999. At the end of the first decade of the twenty-first century, Israel and Cyprus followed the process which was started by Israel. In 2007, the Greek Cypriot government gave production licenses of thirteen for hydrocarbon production zones to international companies (Republic of Turkey Ministry of Foreign Affairs, 2007). In 2009, Israel announced that it was going to open a new field called "Tamar." Following that in the same year, Turkish officials announced that they had already conducted searches in the region. Israel discovered a new region for hydrocarbon in 2010 called "Leviathan." In 2011, Cyprus found a new area called Aphrodite. It was followed by trilateral cooperation among Israel, Greece, and Cyprus, establishing a "New Energy Triangle[2]." In 2012, Turkish officials announced that they would start a discovery license for searching hydrocarbon. In 2012, Cyprus gave a searching license for the second time (Republic of Turkey Ministry of Foreign Affairs, 2012). The next year, Israel found another zone named "Karish." In 2015, Egypt discovered another hydrocarbon zone titled "Zohr."[3] Egypt became a part of the "New Energy Triangle" in 2016. Due to these multiple efforts and hydrocarbon activities, until 2020, the tension in the Eastern Mediterranean has been on a high level.

The initiative called the "EastMed Gas Forum" in January 2020 by Cyprus, Egypt, Greece, Italy, Jordan, and Palestine has been perceived by Turkey as an effort to eliminate and contain Turkey in the Eastern Mediterranean[4]. On the other hand, Greece and RoC, supported by the EU, identified Turkey's activities in the East Mediterranean as illegal and provocative. Although this rising tension and the crisis in the Eastern Mediterranean has perceived as a multilayered and multi-actor problem, the core of the crisis is the Turkish–Greek relations and the Cyprus issue. Yet, dissimilar to the past, which was only a regional competition, a lot more players are engaged in the region politically and militarily. The United States, Russia, France, Egypt, Israel, Cyprus, Italy, and the UAE are among the nation states directing maritime and naval activities in the Eastern Mediterranean.[5]

These activities, which gradually increased in the Eastern Mediterranean, made the Cyprus problem even more complicated. Turkey's activities carried out in the Eastern Mediterranean have been represented as a violation of the sovereign rights of the Republic of Cyprus by Greece and the RoC. They argue that the area where Turkey conducts drilling and research activities is the proclaimed EEZ of the RoC. On the other hand, Turkey does not recognize the Republic of Cyprus and its EEZ. Moreover, Turkey frequently advocates the rights of Turkish Cypriots on the resources found and will be found.

It can be stated that increasing activities, increasing number of actors, and overlapping economic and national interests in the Eastern Mediterranean have been linked to the Cyprus problem and worsened the relations between Turkey and Greece. Thus, the rapprochement period that started in 1999 and resulted in an increased density of interaction in many aspects has come to an end. The endurance of the rapprochement between Turkey and Greece began to be questioned since the 2010s. Türkeş-Kılıç, in her study that analyzes the official statements of both countries issued in the second half of the rapprochement, argues that "in the 2010s, Turkey and Greece have addressed each other mostly on security issues."[6] The conflict over the East Med region is not the only reason for this disengagement; there are also other issues such as the migration crisis and the Aegean disputes. However, this crisis shows us the fragility of Turkish–Greek conciliation and the significance of the long history of rivalry and consolidated enmity in shaping bilateral relations.

The main purpose of this chapter is to analyze the impact of the energy crisis in the Eastern Mediterranean Region on the bilateral relations of Turkey and Greece. While doing so, the official statements of Turkish and Greek Foreign Ministries were scrutinized. At first, the statements including the keywords "energy, hydrocarbon, and Eastern Mediterranean" are collected. Then by utilizing an online word frequency program, the frequency of the words used in the statements was counted. We prepared tables that show "word frequency" and how many times each word appears in the statements. Finding the most frequent phrases and words enables us to understand the most significant issues and priorities for the Foreign Ministries of both countries. As a second step, we utilize a discourse analysis that is sometimes defined as the analysis of language "beyond the sentence."[7]

Greece has 128 statements including the words "energy, hydrocarbon, and Eastern Mediterranean." The first statement was issued on April 4, 2011. Turkey has issued a total of forty-six statements. The first release was made on January 30, 2007. In this study, 174 statements of Turkey and Greece were scrutinized. All of the statements are derived from the official websites of Turkish and Greek Foreign Ministries.

STATEMENTS OF TURKEY

In the scope of this research, the Republic of Turkey's Ministry of Foreign Affairs' statements that included certain keywords were analyzed: Eastern Mediterranean, hydrocarbon, and energy. In this context, the first accessible statement is from 2007. Since 2007, Turkey, in its statements regarding the East Mediterranean, has emphasized the Turkish Republic of Northern Cyprus and the rights of Turkish Cypriots.

As shown in Table 5.1, "Cyprus" has been the most frequently used phrase in the statements of the Turkish Foreign Ministry. Thus, it can be stated that, according to Turkey, the Eastern Mediterranean issue is directly linked to the Cyprus question. The situation remains similar when we consider the word frequency as "two words." The terms "Greek Cypriots" and "Turkish Cypriots" are among the most frequently used expressions in the official statements of Turkey. Discourse analysis utilized supports the information in Table 5.1. Turkey frequently emphasizes that the Turkish Cypriots, like the Greek Cypriots, have equal and indivisible rights over the natural resources of the entire continental shelf of the island.

Turkey, in its statement dated January 2007, explained that "In Eastern Mediterranean, which can be considered a half-closed sea, continental shelf or EEZ restrictions are only possible with arrangements that protect the interests of all parties and that are agreed upon by all interested countries" and stressed the importance of fair sharing of resources in the Eastern Mediterranean.[8]

Again in the same statement, the agreements of the Greek Cypriot administration of Southern Cyprus (GCASC)[9] with Egypt and Lebanon were criticized and through highlighting that the Turkish Republic of Northern Cyprus (TRNC) also has rights and authority over the island of Cyprus' marine areas, Turkey indicated that GCASC does not represent the whole island.[10]

In addition to the aforementioned statement, the agreements of GCASC with Egypt and Lebanon were castigated by Turkey. Furthermore, by expressing that Turkish Cypriots are "the other founding people of the Island," it is emphasized that the rights of both Turkish Cypriots and the Republic of Turkey in the Eastern Mediterranean will be protected.

The statement made in August, 2007 by the Republic of Turkey's Ministry of Foreign Affairs expressed that its opinions regarding the GCASC's attempts against international law and legitimacy to restrict maritime jurisdictions and issue oil/natural gas exploration licenses in the Eastern Mediterranean are announced to the world public on every occasion in all relevant international organizations, including the UN. In the same statement, by underlining the necessity of joint utilization of the resources of the island

Table 5.1 Most frequently used terms

Turkey 2007		*Words and Frequency*	
One Word	*Frequency*	*Two Words*	*Frequency*
Cyprus	13	Eastern Mediterranean	4
Turkey	6	Cyprus Island	4
Lebanon	5	Greek Cypriot	3
Turkey 2009		Words and Frequency	
One Word	Frequency	Two Words	Frequency
Turkey	4	Eastern Mediterranean	3
Research	3	Turkey's Oil	2
Turkey 2010		Words and Frequency	
One Word	Frequency	Two Words	Frequency
Cyprus	12	Comprehensive Solution	3
Israel	4	Turkish Cypriot	3
Solution	4	Eastern Mediterranean	2
Turkey 2011		Words and Frequency	
One Word	Frequency	Two Words	Frequency
Cyprus	12	Continental Shelf	4
TRNC	10	Comprehensive Solution	4
Turkey	6	Eastern Mediterranean	3
Turkey 2012		Words and Frequency	
One Word	Frequency	Two Words	Frequency
Cyprus	15	Turkish Cypriot	8
TRNC	12	Hydrocarbon Search	4
Turkey	10	International Oil	3
Turkey 2013		Words and Frequency	
One Word	Frequency	Two Words	Frequency
Cyprus	11	Turkish Cypriot	8
Turkey	11	Natural Resources	4
Cypriot	7	Greek Side	3
Turkey 2014		Words and Frequency	
One Word	Frequency	Two Words	Frequency
Cyprus	22	Greek Cypriot	6
Greek	15	Turkish Side	6
Turkey	11	Turkish Cypriot6	6
Turkey 2016		Words and Frequency	
One Word	Frequency	Two Words	Frequency
Cyprus	7	Hydrocarbon Search	3
Hydrocarbon	4	Turkis Cypriot	3
Greek	3	International Hydrocarbon	2
Turkey 2017		Words and Frequency	
One Word	Frequency	Two Word	Frequency
Cyprus	33	Turkish Cypriot	14

(*Continued*)

Table 5.1 Most frequently used terms *(Continued)*

Turkey 2007		*Words and Frequency*	
One Word	*Frequency*	*Two Words*	*Frequency*
Greek	18	Greek Cypriot	9
Turkish	16	Greek Administration	8
Turkey 2018		Words and Frequency	
One Word	Frequency	Two Words	Frequency
Cyprus	60	Turkish Cypriot	26
Turkish	31	Eastern Mediterranean	20
Greek	25	Unilateral	11
Turkey 2019		Words and Frequency	
One Word	Frequency	Two Words	Frequency
Cyprus	153	Eastern Mediterranean	52
Turkey	72	Turkish Cypriot	32
International	41	Greek Cypriot	18

by Turkish Cypriots and Greek Cypriots, the importance of finding a fair, durable, and comprehensive solution is stressed.

It is indicated that Turkey will not accept the attempts of GCASC to restrict maritime jurisdictions, and Turkey also has legitimate rights and authority over maritime areas on the West of Cyprus Island, especially starting from 32° 16′ 18″ east longitude.[11]

In the statement dated July 2009, it is announced that the Turkish Petroleum Corporation (TPC) carried out geophysical research activities between November 14 and 18, 2008, within the maritime jurisdiction areas of Turkey in the eastern Mediterranean.[12]

In a statement made in December 2010, it is expressed that it is worrying to see the Greek Cypriot administration of Southern Cyprus (GCASC) make bilateral agreements with countries in East Mediterranean about maritime jurisdictions since 2003.

In a statement made in the aftermath of GCASC signing an EEZ restriction agreement with Israel in December 2010, it is emphasized that GCASC signing such a deal means ignoring the rights and interests of the Turkish Cypriots, and it will negatively affect the Cyprus negotiations and will not contribute to peace and stability in the East Mediterranean. The same criticism has also been directed at Israel. In the statement, it is expressed that Turkey has no claims over the maritime areas mentioned in the EEZ restriction agreement and Turkey approaches this matter in the context of the Cyprus issue.[13]

In the statement made on August 5, 2011, it is highlighted that the Greek Cypriot side does not have the right and the authority to unilaterally speak, initiate enterprise, and/or sign agreements for the whole island regarding the natural resources that belong to all of the island's population. Additionally, it is explained that these kinds of attempts of GCASC create tension in the island and the region, violate the right of Turkish Cypriots to benefit equally from the natural resources of the island, and harm the ongoing negotiation process.

Turkey's Ministry of Foreign Affairs, who defined the Greek Cypriot administration's unilateral enterprises as an "example of irresponsibility" in its statement, underlined that it is necessary for the international community to not permit the attempts of the Greek Cypriot side to usurp the right of Turkish Cypriots to benefit equally from the natural resources of the island.[14] Since the beginning, Turkey has been evaluating the developments in East Mediterranean about maritime jurisdiction sharing and energy in the context of the Cyprus issue.

Turkey, who has stressed international community and international law in its statement made in 2011, expressed that it will continue its ventures according to international law through diplomatic and strategic channels to protect the legitimate rights and interests of the Turkish Republic of Northern Cyprus (TRNC).[15]

According to the statement dated September 15, 2011, TRNC and Turkey have agreed upon a Continental Shelf Limitation Agreement. Moreover, it is announced that TRNC will give oil and gas exploration and extraction licenses to the TPC in sea areas around the island.

While the efforts of Turkey and TRNC to reach a lasting solution on the Cyprus issue were underlined, it was emphasized that the natural wealth of Cyprus should be shared fairly by the two peoples that are the co-owners of the island.[16]

Turkey's Ministry of Foreign Affairs, who released a statement after the news of GCASC's new international hydrocarbon exploration licenses, described the step taken by Greek Cypriots despite all the warnings as irresponsible, provocative, and one-sided and protested. The international community's attention was drawn to the fact that this initiative of the GCASC violates the equal and natural rights of the Turkish Cypriots, and it is against the purpose and spirit of the ongoing UN comprehensive settlement negotiations and causes tension in the region. It is emphasized that the license areas of the tender opened by GCASC both violate the continental shelf of Turkey and coincide with the license areas given to TPC by TRNC on September 22, 2011.[17]

In the statement made in February 2013, it is reemphasized that the Turkish Cypriots, like the Greek Cypriots, have equal and indivisible rights over the natural resources of the entire continental shelf of the island and it is stated that the two peoples on the island must decide together on how to use the natural gas and oil resources in the sea. It is stated that the companies that collaborate with GCASC despite all the warnings of Turkey will be excluded from all future energy projects of Turkey. Furthermore, if international oil companies operate in the field in question, they will face the TRNC and TPC and undesirable tensions may arise. According to the Ministry's statement, Turkey, in such an event, as previously stated, will give every kind of support to TRNC in its responsibility as the motherland and as the guarantor state.[18]

The statement made in February 2013 is important in the sense that it is addressed to Greece instead of GCASC for the first time. When one looks at the statements done before this date, it can be seen that they were addressed to the Greek Cypriot administration. However, with this statement, Greece became one of the addressees of Turkey in the region. The basis of this statement is Greece carrying the claims that the license granted by Turkey to TPC overlaps with its own continental shelf. According to Turkey, Greece's claims do not have a foothold in international law. Despite this, in the statement made by Turkey, it is underlined that while necessary steps will be taken to protect its sovereign rights, it is determined to continue to develop relations with Greece.[19] With the statement made in March 2013, it is indicated that the GCASC does not have the legitimacy to use the island's natural resources alone, as if it is the sole owner of the island. Turkey expressed that the GCASC would not be allowed to use the economic crisis as an excuse to make a fait accompli in the issue of the island's natural resources. Turkish Cypriots and Southern Cypriots should decide together on the future of the island. Turkey explained that it will always respect the choice of the people of the island. However, it stated that in the Eastern Mediterranean, it will allow a violation of neither its rights nor the rights of the Turkish Cypriot people.[20]

The statement made in October 2014 expresses that Turkey will protect the rights of the Turkish Cypriot side; it is wrong that GCASC is acting like the sole owner of the island, and the problems on the island cannot be solved through ignoring the Turkish Cypriots.[21] The importance of the announcement made in October 2014 is that it is evidence that Turkey perceives the problem as the Cyprus issue. The point that Turkey criticizes the GCASC for is that it did not participate in the settlement negotiation upon their restart. For this reason, Turkey blames the instability and deadlock on the island on GCASC, as it is their primary reason.[22] Referring to the talks between the TRNC and Turkey in November 2014, the subject about which both Turkey and TRNC criticize GCASC is its withdrawal from the negotiations using Turkey's seismic activity in the Eastern Mediterranean as an excuse.[23]

In the statement made in March 2016, Turkey, by criticizing the third hydrocarbon exploration field started by the Greek Cypriot administration, explained that these efforts disregard the rights of Turkey and the Turkish Cypriots and they will negatively affect the resolution and negotiation processes on the island. Additionally, it is stated that hydrocarbon exploration efforts cannot be made only by Greek Cypriots in Cyprus, and international hydrocarbon companies that will participate in this so-called tender should take careful steps to resolve these principles and the problems of the island.[24]

In the light of statements made in May 2017, Turkey condemns the tender of Greek Cypriots and criticizes their approach to resolve the issues on the island by ignoring the Turkish Cypriots and taking only the Greek Cypriots into account, as they have previously done. Moreover, Turkey expresses that it will protect its rights and interests in the Eastern Mediterranean, no matter what the cost is. Turkey also reacts to the Greek Administration's agreement with a few companies about the details of this tender.[25]

In a statement dated April 2017, Turkey, criticizing the third tender made by the Greek Cypriot administration, argues that it includes areas that belong to the continental shelf of Turkish Cypriots. Additionally, it indicates that Turkey will not allow any company, institution, or state to violate the interests of Turkey and the Turkish Cypriots.[26]

In a statement made in December 2017, Turkey showed that in the future TPC will start the seismic activity in the region in accordance with the tender given to it and the Greek Cypriot administration creating a search area within the territory of the continental shelf of Turkey was given as the reason for this development. The Greek Cypriot administration was criticized for distancing itself from resolution and stability on the island, along with its attitude.[27]

In the statement issued in February 2018, the Greek Cypriot administration is accused of endangering the security and stability of the Eastern Mediterranean region by ignoring the stability of Cyprus instead of working for the region's security and stability. The Greek Cypriot administration is declared as the sole responsible party for what happens next. At the same time, it stated that that Greek Cypriots expressed that they do not see themselves as equals with the Turkish Cypriots in the Cyprus conference they organized. It is conveyed that the Greek Cypriot side is far from being constructive, and it is the primary reason for the problems that have existed in the past 50 years.[28]

In the statement dated July 2018, Turkey condemned the statements of the Greek Cypriot administration disregarding the Turkish Cypriot people on the island, hydrocarbon activities, and the ambassadors of the third party states and invited them to remember their positions.[29]

Turkey, in its statement in October 2018, by expressing that it will not give up on its continental shelf in the Eastern Mediterranean and that it will not allow any foreign hydrocarbon exploration company without its permission, and these areas are licensed to Turkey Petroleum Corporation (TPC) emphasized that these areas will not be given to any state or company without Turkey' permission. In the same statement, it is said that the No. 7 research area of the Greek Cypriot administration is within the continental shelf of Turkey that is officially recognized by the UN.[30]

In another statement, Turkey criticized the defense cooperation between GCASC and France and underlined that it is against the 1960 Founding Treaty. Moreover, Turkey indicated that the Greek Cypriot administration, with this move, endangers the stability and security of the Eastern Mediterranean.[31]

In its statement dated May 2019, Turkey explains that it is fully committed to fully protect its legitimate rights based on international law and acts in accordance with these principles. Turkey does not accept the accusations against it, claiming that it is raising the tension and states that the only side to blame is the Greek Cypriot administration as it is acting as if it is the sole owner of the island.[32] In the statement made in June 2019, Turkey accused the Greek Cypriot administration of seeing itself as the only owner of the island and ignoring the Turkish Cypriots. This accusation is based on the Greek side not leaving any right to live to the Turkish Cypriots. It is stated that, along with the administration of the island, in subjects like natural gas and oil, Greek and Turkish Cypriots should be equal. Turkey reported that TPC is researching in there with the license given to it in 2011.[33]

In June 2019, Turkey stated that it thinks that the decisions are taken in the Conference of EU Member Southern European Countries and the statements made in it are unfortunate and against the law. Turkey expressed that the EU is an unreliable institution, and it is unacceptable for it to act as a court. By explaining that the Greek Cypriot administration is the reason for the economic and political instability in the Eastern Mediterranean, Turkey indicated that the Greek side does not want a resolution on the island, and the EU is also involved in this.[34]

Upon the accusations of Greece and the Greek Cypriot administration, Turkey issued a statement in July 2019 expressing that GCASC entered the EU illegally and defined Greece as the "spoiled child of Europe." As for the GCASC, Turkey accused it of destabilizing the Eastern Mediterranean and defined it as the "Naughty child of Europe." Through saying these, Turkey indicated that accusations made against it actually belong to these two EU Member states. Moreover, Turkey stated that being an EU Member will not legitimize GCASC usurping the legitimate rights and interests of the Turkish Cypriots. It is also said that Turkey will protect the rights and interests of the Turkish Cypriots as well as its own.[35]

The statement made in July 2019 is important in the sense that it explained the significance of hydrocarbon activities in the Eastern Mediterranean. Turkey not only conveyed that in the Eastern Mediterranean, the Greek Cypriot side is not willing to agree, and it is the primary reason why events have escalated to this level but also based its hydrocarbon activities in the Eastern Mediterranean on two bases. The first one is the continental shelf rights of Turkey, and the second one is the Cyprus issue. In this statement, Turkey stresses that its movements are entirely in accordance with international law and expresses that it is useless for GCASC to try to solve the EEC issue before the current problem on the island. Turkey explains that the reason for this is because it is impossible and wrong to decide on EEC without resolving the issue on the whole island and establishing a governance structure that will represent the entire island population. Turkey also states that, if GCASC continues with these wrongdoings, Turkey and Turkish Cypriots will continue their policies on hydrocarbon with determination.[36]

In the statement dated September 2019, Turkey affirms that the area declared by GCASC, who ignored the Turkish Cypriots, as the No. 7 Research area is within Turkey's continental shelf as recorded by the UN and the participation of Italian ENI and French Total companies, which agreed here, in this tender is invalid. Turkey expressed that no foreign company or state can conduct research here without permission, and this decision will continue with determination. Turkey further stated that the hydrocarbon research of GCASC is done against the rights of Turkish Cypriots, and Turkey's offer to share the hydrocarbon resources around the island equally is still valid. It is also explained that as long as the GCASC does not consider this, it risks the security and stability of the Eastern Mediterranean.[37]

In its statement issued in September 2019, Turkey expressed that the statements made in the meeting of Egypt, Greece, and GCASC in New York are insincere and totally outside of reality. Turkey accused Greece and GCASC of endangering the security of the region. Turkey evaluates the statement of Greece as insincere and unwarranted because while Greece states that it is always ready to open dialogue with Turkey, it is trying to find alliances. Turkey accused these countries of ignoring Turkey and Turkish Cypriots in the Eastern Mediterranean[38].

Turkey, in its statement dated October 2019, expressed that resolutions that are according to international law and based on equity can create lasting solutions. Turkey accused Greece and GCASC of being unjust. Turkey indicated that for the resolution of issues they are willing to meet with anyone except for GCASC. Furthermore, Turkey explained that the reason why it does not accept GCASC as an interlocutor is that Turkey sees it as at the same level as the Turkish Cypriots.[39]

In the statement made in November 2019, Turkey expressed that it considers the decisions taken by the EU to be unlawful and unwarranted. Turkey affirms that it sees the hydrocarbon activities of Turkey and Turkish Cypriots since 2004 not as factors detrimental to the stability and security but as beneficial to them. The steps were taken in this principle as Greece and GCASC were seen as factors that decrease stability and security. Turkey further indicated that the EU is following a wrong policy by falling into their game.[40]

As for the statements made in December 2019, it is expressed that the maritime jurisdiction agreement signed between Turkey and Libya is based on equity and it definitely cannot be accused justly. About unfairness, Turkey tried to refute the accusations of Greece by expressing that the maritime jurisdiction Greece claims on the island of Meis is 4,000 times more than its surface area. Turkey, with this agreement it signed with Libya, tried to show that not only itself but also other Eastern Mediterranean countries are disturbed by the policies of Greece and GCASC.[41]

STATEMENTS OF GREECE

In the scope of this research, Greece's Ministry of Foreign Affairs' statements that included certain keywords were analyzed: Eastern Mediterranean, Hydrocarbon, and Energy. In this context, the first accessible statement is from 2011.

As shown in Table 5.2, "Cyprus, energy, and cooperation" have been the most frequently used terms until 2018. Since 2018, most of the statements issued by the Greek Foreign Ministry have addressed Turkey and Turkey's actions in the region. The year 2019 has been a significant turning point in terms of the number of statements and the frequency of "Turkey" in the declarations. The situation remains similar when we consider the word frequency as "two words." The term "international law" is among the most frequently used expressions in the official statements of Greece. The utilized discourse analysis supports the information in the table above. Greece frequently emphasizes that Turkey violates international law; on the contrary, Greece is a country that respects international law.

The first statements of the Greek Foreign Ministry emphasized the sovereign rights of the Republic of Cyprus[42] by avoiding an accusatory tone toward Turkey. Most of the statements criticized Turkey's actions and announcements that disclaim Cyprus' exploitation activities and exercises.

In a statement dated October 2011, the then foreign minister Lambrinidis stated that "the recent actions and statements from Turkey—concerning the Republic of Cyprus's exercising of its sovereign right to move ahead to the exploitation of its natural wealth—obviously conflict with international law."[43] A year later, the then foreign minister Avramopoulos criticized Turkey's position toward the Republic of Cyprus's extraction of hydrocarbons and calls them "Turkey's unacceptable threats against Cypriot activities."[44]

When the statements of the Greek Foreign Ministry are analyzed, it can be argued that Greece frequently declares its support for Turkey's membership in the European Union. However, this support is constantly accompanied by criticism toward Turkey concerning the Cyprus issue or the East Med. Especially after 2018, Greece emphasizes its European identity more than ever and uses it as leverage against Turkey. In most of the statements, Greece

Table 5.2 Most frequently used terms

Greece 2011		*Words and Frequency*	
One Word	*Frequency*	*Two Words*	*Frequency*
Energy	30	Natural Gas	15
Greece	30	Security Council	4
Gas	22	Energy Policy	3
Greece 2012		Words and Frequency	
One Word	Frequency	Two Words	Frequency
Energy	18	Cyprus Issue	4
Cyprus	12	Nuclear Energy	3
Hydrocarbons	7	Nuclear Power	3
Greece 2013		Words and Frequency	
One Word	Frequency	Two Words	Frequency
Cyprus	29	Cyprus Issue	8
Greece	17	Continental Shelf	6
Law	12	International Law	3
Greece 2014		Words and Frequency	
One Word	Frequency	Two Words	Frequency
Cyprus	58	Sovereign Rights	14
International	31	International Law	12
Greece	30	Continental Shelf	11
Greece 2015		Words and Frequency	
One Word	Frequency	Two Words	Frequency
Cooperation	27	Trilateral Summit	7
Cyprus	16	Middle East	6
Security	16	Eastern Mediterranean	6
Greece 2016		Words and Frequency	
One Word	Frequency	Two Words	Frequency
Cooperation	14	International Law	5
Energy	11	Secretary General	4
Cyprus	9	Foreign Affairs	3
Greece 2017		Words and Frequency	
One Word	Frequency	Two Words	Frequency
Cyprus	4		
Hydrocarbons	2		
Greece 2018		Words and Frequency	
One Word	Frequency	Two Words	Frequency
Energy	16	International Law	7
Cyprus	15	Eastern Mediterranean	6
Turkey	12	Turkish Side	6
Greece 2019		Words and Frequency	
One Word	Frequency	Two Words	Frequency
Turkey	334	Eastern Mediterranean	128
Greece	303	International Law	113
International	220	European Union	111

portrays itself as a European country that wholeheartedly follows international law, democracy, and good neighborly relations.

For example, in a statement dated February 2014, the then minister of Foreign Affairs Venizelos stated that Greece is in favor of Turkey's European perspective and wants "a Turkey that is stable, prosperous, trustworthy; a Turkey that does not export crises."[45]

Beginning in 2016, even though it is not caustic as in 2019, the tone of the Greek statements toward Turkey became bitter. Greece starts to call Turkey's rhetoric "threatening" and calls Turkey to show respect to "inalienable rights of the sovereign Republic of Cyprus."[46]

In February 2018, the then foreign minister Kotzias, by referring the naval exercises of Turkey, stated that "Turkey is illegally interfering, through naval exercises, in a foreign EEZ." In other words, he blamed Turkey for violating the EEZ of the Republic of Cyprus and the International Law of the Sea.[47] One month later, Kotzias, while indicating the interests of the Republic of Cyprus, announced that Turkey's conducts threatens not only RoC but also the vital interests of the EU.[48] When the official statements of the Greek Foreign Ministry are considered, it can be stated that since 2018 there is a significant emphasis on the rights and the role of the European Union in the dispute.

In December 2018, during the Trilateral Summit, Israel, Egypt, and Greece reiterated their "full support and solidarity with the Republic of Cyprus in exercising its sovereign rights in its Exclusive Economic Zone." They declared that "any attempt to violate these rights in a manner that will endanger the stability of the Eastern Mediterranean and the Aegean Sea, violate international law, or contradict good neighborly relations."[49] This Summit manifested concrete cooperation and solidarity among those countries. The then Greek prime minister Alexis Tsipras declared that their "objective is, within this partnership, to also include other countries in the future. And other countries of the region with energy resources." He mentioned that they "do not want to exclude anyone." It can be stated that a more moderate approach toward Turkey was taken by the then government of Greece in late 2018.[50]

However, in January 2019, Tsipras stated that "the relations with Turkey, and the EU as a whole, must be based on mutual respect and, above all, on respect of International Law." In his speech, Tsipras underlined that "Turkey must respect International Law, both in the Eastern Mediterranean, as well as in the Aegean."[51] In February, during his visit to Turkey, Tsipras stressed the significance of cooperation between Turkey and Greece and stated that "energy should serve as a bridge and not as an obstacle, not as a subject of conflict in the region." He also emphasized the significance of "respecting international law in the Mediterranean plays," as in his previous statement.[52]

The then minister of Foreign Affairs Giorgos Katrougalos, during his meeting with his Turkish counterpart Çavuşoğlu, stated that the Greek position is "a position deriving from International Law of the Sea," and declared that "the Greek side will continue to act precisely within this framework."[53]

After the beginning of Turkey's drilling activities in the Mediterranean, the tone of the statements has changed dramatically. In April, the then Ministry of Foreign Affairs Katrougalos calls Turkey an "isolated country which projects power in order to create faits accomplis." In the same speech, he argued that Greece's actions are based on international law, while Turkish activities are "illegal."[54]

Again, in May 2019, he called Turkey's drilling activities "illegal" and announced that "Turkey should immediately cease its illegal activities, to respect the inalienable rights of the sovereign Republic of Cyprus exercised in the interests of all Cypriot people."[55]

Also, alternate minister of Foreign Affairs Sia Anagnostopoulou called Turkey's drilling activities "Turkey's provocativeness."[56] Moreover, the then president Pavlopoulos, by portraying Greece as a country of guarantor of International and European Law, accused Turkey to be "an arrogant and ignorant actor who confuses might is right."[57]

In June 2019, Anagnostopoulou, the then alternate minister of Foreign Affairs, declared that "Greece is sincerely and firmly in favor of Turkey's accession to the European Union. However, there is a fear that Turkey is pulling away from its European perspective with its provocative conduct in the Aegean and Eastern Mediterranean." She portrayed Turkey as an actor who "jeopardizes not only region's security, but also Europe's."[58] Also, in a statement dated June 2019, the then minister of Foreign Affairs, Katrougalos, blamed Turkey with very similar arguments such as being "a neighbor who is pursuing a strategy of revisionism, trying to dispute international law with provocative acts." On the other hand, he frequently emphasizes "Greece's respect for international legality."[59]

In another statement, Katrougalos argued that "Turkey's escalating provocations in Cyprus and the continued tension in the Aegean are not a show of strength, but one of weakness." According to him, "Turkish policy is marked by perennial elements of hegemony, that evokes memories of the Ottoman Empire. Also, Turkish policy against Greece is its revisionist strategy against international conventions and especially the Law of the Sea". He also defined Greek foreign policy as "a foreign policy that is based on respecting international law."[60]

In an interview dated June 2019, Anagnostopoulou, by referring to the decision taken by the European Union to impose sanctions on Turkey, stated that Turkey is "practising illegal drilling activities in the Cypriot EEZ, and trampling the sovereign rights of a member state of the European Union."[61]

Similarly, Katrougalos indicated the European Council Decision of March 2018, which clearly condemned Turkey's actions in the Aegean and the Eastern Mediterranean as violations of international legality. He also called Turkey as a revisionist state who involves in illegal conduct in the Eastern Mediterranean region.[62]

In another interview dated June 2019, Katrougalos, while addressing Greek citizens, stated that "Greeks should feel safe because Greece's voice is strong and respected." He argues that "the strategy of revisionism of international agreements is a consistent characteristic of Turkey's policy. Turkey has always felt suffocated by the rules of international law." By referring the deteriorated Turkish–US relations, he states that "Greece fill the strategic gap left by Turkey." He also emphasized that Turkey is internationally isolated and losing its diplomatic capital, "the longer Ankara persists, the more it will lose, rather than gain."[63] In a statement dated June 2019, the then minister of Foreign Affairs Katrougalos portrayed Turkey as a country "isolated, provocative, and clearly loosing." He stated that "while Turkey is losing, Greece and RoC are making gains." According to him, "Turkey's provocative moves are not indicative of power, but of weakness."[64]

Beginning in 2019, the tones of the statements of the Greek Foreign Ministry became very accusing. Every action of Turkey started to be interpreted as hostile, provocative, and illegal. Katrougalos frequently mentioned that Greece and RoC are gaining ground and becoming stronger, while Turkey is losing its credibility. For example, in June 2019, Katrougalos stated that "never before has Greece's voice been so strong and respected on the European and international stage. Never before has Turkey been so diplomatically isolated."[65] In most of the statements, the Greek Foreign Ministry condemned Turkey and calls its drilling activities as illegal and violation of international law and the rights of the RoC.

In July 2019, the center-right New Democracy Party won the elections and formed the new government of Greece. Nikos Dendias, former minister of Defense (November 2014 to January 2015), was appointed as the minister of Foreign Affairs. As soon as he took the office, in a statement dated July 2019, he stated that "Greece condemns Turkey's illegal activities in Cyprus's territorial waters and in the Cypriot EEZ." Dendias declared that "Greece's relations with Turkey should be based on international law, the Law of the Sea and good neighborly relations."[66]

In the same month, Dendias paid a visit to the United States where he called Turkish conducts as "Turkish aggression", both towards Cyprus, the sovereignty and sovereign rights of the Republic of Cyprus, and towards Greece's sovereign rights in the wider region of the Aegean Sea and the Eastern Mediterranean. He also asked the United States to adopt a clear position to support Greece about issues, what he calls "Turkish aggression."[67]

In another statement dated August 2019, alternate minister of Foreign Affairs, Varvitsiotis, presented the basis of Greece's Cyprus policy as "Nicosia decides, Greece follows." He called Turkey's activities in the region "provocations" and emphasized Greece's strategic alliance with Israel and Egypt.[68] According to Varvitsiotis, Greece is a pillar of stability and security in the Southeastern Mediterranean that wants to maintain good neighborly relations with Turkey. To realize this, Turkey should respect international law and European borders.[69]

In a statement dated October 2019, Dendias declared that Greece will not let East Mediterranean return to the era of "gunboat diplomacy." He stated that Turkey is isolating itself from the rest of the region with its provocative actions and turning itself as a "troublemaker" in the region.[70]

In the month, in another statement, Dendias called Turkey's actions "foolish actions contrary to the international law." He stated that "Greece wants Turkey to come closer to the West which represents the ideas that developed after the Enlightenment and encompasses democracy, human rights, tolerance towards diversity, the concept of protection of citizens." He argues that Turkey intentionally raises the tension in the region to force the United States and the EU to mediate the dispute as in the 1990s, so that Turkey can gain from tensions and conflict.[71]

In an interview dated December 2019, Dendias criticized President Erdoğan and his government to use the tension and the dispute in the region as a tool to boost their popularity within Turkey. He argues that Turkey, contrary to the "Zero Problems with the Neighbours" policy initiated by Davutoğlu, "managed to have problems on all of its borders." He also states that Greece does not want to resolve conflicts through military means, but it is capable of defending its national territory. Dendias, referring to the European identity of Greece, affirmed that Greece is a country that respects international law.[72]

Dendias and the statements issued by the Hellenic Foreign Ministry frequently indicated the European identity of Greece as a superior feature against Turkey. They defined Turkey as a country with unlawful actions, far from the European values, and a provocative actor who tries to create troubles in the region. According to the statements, Turkey ought to copy Greece who is a model country of stability respecting international law, maintaining good relations with the other countries in the region. For example, in a statement dated December 2019, Dendias argued that "Greece is a European country. Turkey will not drag us down to the level of Balkan brawler."[73] Here, Turkey is openly associated with troubles and disputes. In the last statement of 2019, Dendias have taken a more severe tone against Turkey by referring to Greece's allies and military capabilities. He calls Turkey as "reckless and isolated" actor who intentionally provokes a heated incident and increases the tension.[74]

CONCLUSION

In this study, the statements of the Ministry of Foreign Affairs of Turkey and Greece between 2007 and 2019 are analyzed to understand the impact of the developments in the Eastern Mediterranean Region on the bilateral relations of Turkey and Greece. In this context, the official statements, those containing the keywords "energy, hydrocarbon, and Eastern Mediterranean," were included in the analysis. While Turkey's first official release was in 2007, Greece's first official statement was issued in 2011.

As for Turkey, in most of the statements, Turkey accuses Greek Cypriots of seeing themselves as the only owner of the island and ignoring the rights of the Turkish Cypriots. Turkey emphasizes that the natural wealth of Cyprus should be shared fairly by the two peoples that are the co-owners of the island. According to Turkey, Turkish Cypriots and their rights cannot be disregarded, and Turkish Cypriots and Greek Cypriots should decide together on the future of the island. As in the cooperation between Greece and the Greek Cypriots, Turkey states that it will give every kind of support to TRNC in its responsibility as the motherland and as the guarantor state. Turkey argues that the Greek Cypriots entered the EU illegally without reaching a final solution on the island. Turkey portrays Greece as the "spoiled child of Europe" and accuses Greek Cypriots of destabilizing the Eastern Mediterranean and defines them as "Naughty children of Europe."

Greece, particularly since 2019, emphasizes Turkey's diplomatic isolation. According to Greece, Turkey is a country which is isolated and constantly losing ground and credibility. For example, in a statement, by referring to the United States, it is argued that Greece fills the strategic gap left by Turkey. While Greece states that it stands by the Republic of Cyprus at every opportunity, it underlines the diplomatic achievements they succeed in together. Greece portrays itself as a country that respects international law, successful in the diplomatic sphere, and able to establish strong alliances. They define themselves as a full-fledged democracy and a model country in the region. Greece repeatedly stresses that the Republic of Cyprus is a member of the European Union and argues that Turkey, with its unlawful actions, also violates the borders of the European Union. Greece's policy toward the issue is based on the principle of "Nicosia decides, Greece follows." Greece constantly reiterates its full support and solidarity with the Republic of Cyprus in exercising its sovereign rights in its EEZ.

The analysis gives us signs about the state of Turkish–Greek relations and the current stalemate in the Cyprus issue. Turkey's statements, instead of Greece, mostly address the Greek Cypriots and the European Union. Greece mentions Turkey in almost all of the statements related to the issue. Turkey sees the problem within the framework of the fair distribution of resources that belongs to Cyprus among Turkish and Greek Cypriots. On the other hand, Greece regards the issue as a violation of the sovereignty of the Republic of Cyprus by Turkey.

In addition to the different perspectives that make the issue more complicated, the diversity of the actors involved and the EU's unconditional support to Greece and the RoC decrease the hopes for reconciliation. It can be stated that Turkish–Greek relations are also in an impasse due to the Eastern Mediterranean crisis. By analyzing the statements, we observe that both countries, although they are more on the Greek side, make serious allegations to each other. This reveals that the rapprochement between Turkey and Greece is very fragile due to the historical enmity and consolidated negative images. With an emerging crisis, these negative perceptions and stereotypes immediately become apparent. Thus, it becomes even more difficult to solve both the current problem and the historical questions between the two countries.

NOTES

1. Michael Tanchum "How Did the Eastern Mediterranean Become the Eye of a Geopolitical Storm?" *Foreign Policy*, August 20, 2020, https://foreignpolicy.com/2020/08/18/eastern-mediterranean-greece-turkey-warship-geopolitical-showdown/.
2. Emre İşeri, Panagiotis Andrikopoulos, "Energy Geopolitics of the Eastern Mediterranean: Will Aphrodite's Lure Fuel Peace in Cyprus?" *Middle Eastern Analysis* 5, no. 51 (Spring 2013): 38.
3. Emre İşeri, " Turkey's Entangled (Energy) Security Concerns and the Cyprus Question in the Eastern Mediterranean," in *Greece and Turkey in Conflict and Cooperation: From Europeanization to De-Europeanization*, ed. Alexis Heraclides, Gizem Alioğlu Çakmak (NewYork: Routledge, 2019), 270.
4. Özgür Ünlühisarcıklı "Turkey Disrupts What It Perceives as Maximalist Greek Policy," The German Marshall Fund of the United States, August 28, 2020, https://www.gmfus.org/blog/2020/08/28/eastern-mediterranean-brinkmanship-clear-and-present-danger#utm_source=Twitter&utm_medium=Social).
5. Ian Lesser, "Eastern Mediterranean Brinkmanship Is a Clear and Present Danger," The German Marshall Fund of the United States, August 28, 2020, https://www.gmfus.org/blog/2020/08/28/eastern-mediterranean-brinkmanship-clear-and-present-danger#utm_source=Twitter&utm_medium=Social.
6. Selin Türkeş-Kılıç, "Accessing the Rapprochement in its Second Decade: A Critical Approach to the Official Discourse between Turkey and Greece," In *Greece and Turkey in Conflict and Cooperation: From Europeanization to De-Europeanization*, ed. Alexis Heraclides, Gizem Alioğlu Çakmak (NewYork: Routledge, 2019), 189.
7. "Discourse Analysis—What Speakers Do in Conversation," Linguistic Society of America, accessed September 22, 2020, https://www.linguisticsociety.org/resource/discourse-analysis-what-speakers-do-conversation/.

8. "30 January 2007, Press Release Regarding the efforts of the Greek Cypriot administration of Southern Cyprus to sign bilateral agreements concerning maritime jurisdiction areas with the countries in the Eastern Mediterranean," Republic of Turkey Ministry of Foreign Affairs, accessed September 21, 2020, http://www.mfa.gov.tr/_p_30-january-2007_-press-release-regarding-the-efforts-of-the-greek-cypriot-administration-of-southern-cyprus-to-sign-bilateral-agreements-concerning-maritime-jurisdiction-areas-with-the-countries-in-the-eastern-mediterranean_br___p_.en.mfa.

9. We use the name "Greek Cypriot administration of Southern Cyprus (GCASC)" in translation, adhering to the original statements of Turkish Ministry of Foreign Affairs.

10. "30 January 2007, Press Release Regarding the efforts of the Greek Cypriot administration of Southern Cyprus to sign bilateral agreements concerning maritime jurisdiction areas with the countries in the Eastern Mediterranean," Republic of Turkey Ministry of Foreign Affairs, accessed September 21, 2020, http://www.mfa.gov.tr/_p_30-january-2007_-press-release-regarding-the-efforts-of-the-greek-cypriot-administration-of-southern-cyprus-to-sign-bilateral-agreements-concerning-maritime-jurisdiction-areas-with-the-countries-in-the-eastern-mediterranean_br___p_.en.mfa.

11. "QA:32—Statement of the Spokesman of the Ministry of Foreign Affairs of Turkey in Response to a Question," Republic of Turkey Ministry of Foreign Affairs, accessed September 21, 2020, http://www.mfa.gov.tr/_p_qa_32---statement-of-the-spokesman-of-the-ministry-of-foreign-affairs-of-turkey-in-response-to-a-question-_unofficial-translation___p_.en.mfa.

12. "SC:20, 28 July 2009, The answer of The Ministry of Foreign Affair's Spokesperson to a Question," Republic of Turkey Ministry of Foreign Affairs, accessed September 21, 2020, http://www.mfa.gov.tr/qa_20_-28-july-2009_-statement-of-the-spokesman-of-the-ministry-of-foreign-affairs-of-turkey-in-response-to-a-question.en.mfa.

13. "No: 288, 21 December 2010, Regarding the EEZ Agreement Signed between GCASC and Israel," Republic of Turkey Ministry of Foreign Affairs, accessed September 21, 2020, http://www.mfa.gov.tr/no_-288_-21-december-2010_-press-release-regarding-the-exclusive-economic-zone-_eez_-delimitation-agreement--signed-between-greek-cypriot-administration-and-israel.en.mfa.

14. "No: 181, 5 August 2011, Regarding the GCASC's Oil and Gas Exploration Activities in the Eastern Mediterranean," Republic of Turkey Ministry of Foreign Affairs, accessed September 21, 2020, http://www.mfa.gov.tr/no_-181_-5-august-2011_-press-release-regarding-the-greek-cypriot-administration_s-gas-exploration-activities-in-the-eastern-mediterranean.en.mfa.

15. "No: 181, 5 August 2011, Regarding the GCASC's Oil and Gas Exploration Activities in the Eastern Mediterranean," Republic of Turkey Ministry of Foreign Affairs, accessed September 21, 2020, http://www.mfa.gov.tr/no_-181_-5-august-2011_-press-release-regarding-the-greek-cypriot-administration_s-gas-exploration-activities-in-the-eastern-mediterranean.en.mfa.

16. "No: 216, 21 September 2011 Turkey—TRNC Press Statement Regarding Signing of TRNC Continental Shelf Limitation Agreement of Ministry of Foreign

Affairs," Republic of Turkey Ministry of Foreign Affairs, accessed September 21, 2020, http://www.mfa.gov.tr/no_-216_-21-september-2011_-press-statement-on-the-continental-shelf-delimitation-agreement-signed-between-turkey-and-the-trnc.en.mfa.

17. "No: 43, 15 February 2012, Second International Hydrocarbon Exploration Tender Opened by Southern Cyprus," Republic of Turkey Ministry of Foreign Affairs, accessed September 21, 2020, http://www.mfa.gov.tr/no_-43_-15-february-2012_-second-international-tender-for-off_shore-hydrocarbon-exploration-called-by-the-greek-cypriot-administration-_gca_.en.mfa.

18. "No: 140, 18 May 2012, Regarding the Second International Hydrocarbon Exploration Tender Opened by the GCASC," Republic of Turkey Ministry of Foreign Affairs, accessed September 21, 2020, http://www.mfa.gov.tr/no_-140_-18-may-2012_-press-release-regarding-the-international-tender-for-off_shore-hydrocarbon-exploration-and-exploitation-opened-by-the-greek-cypriot-administration.en.mfa.

19. "No: 46, 22 February 2013, Regarding the Declaration of Greece to the United Nations," Republic of Turkey Ministry of Foreign Affairs, accessed September 21, 2020, http://www.mfa.gov.tr/no_-46_-22-february-2013_-press-release-regarding-the-declaration-of-greece-to-the-united-nations.en.mfa.

20. "No: 83, 23 March 2013 Regarding the Claims of the GCASC on Hydrocarbon Resources in the Eastern Mediterranean," Republic of Turkey Ministry of Foreign Affairs, accessed September 21, 2020, http://www.mfa.gov.tr/no_-83_-23-march-2013_-statement-regarding-the-claims-of-the-gcasc-on-hydrocarbon-resources-in-the-eastern-mediterranean.en.mfa.

21. "No: 311, 04 October 2014, Regarding the Drilling Activities of GASC," Republic of Turkey Ministry of Foreign Affairs, accessed September 21, 2020, http://www.mfa.gov.tr/no_-311_-04-october-2014_-press-release-regarding-drilling-activity-of-the-greek-cypriots.en.mfa.

22. No: 313, 08 October 2014, "Regarding the Decision of the Greek Cypriot Party not to Participate in the Negotiations in the UN Negotiation Process," Republic of Turkey Ministry of Foreign Affairs, accessed September 21, 2020, http://www.mfa.gov.tr/no_-313_-08-october-2014_-press-release-regarding-the-decision-of-the-greek-cypriot-administration-not-to-participate-in-the-discussions-of-the-un-negotiation-process.en.mfa.

23. 25 November 2014, "Prime Minister Davutoğlu met with the TRNC Prime Minister," Republic of Turkey Ministry of Foreign Affairs, accessed September 21, 2020, http://www.mfa.gov.tr/prime-minister-davutoglu-met-with-the-prime-minister-of-trnc.en.mfa.

24. "No: 74, 25 March 2016, Regarding the Third International Hydrocarbon Exploration Tender Opened by the GASC," Republic of Turkey Ministry of Foreign Affairs, accessed September 21, 2020, http://www.mfa.gov.tr/no_-74_-25-march-2016_-press-release-regarding-the-third-international-tender-for-off_shore-hydrocarbon-exploration-by-the-greek-cypriot-administration.en.mfa.

25. "QA-18, 24 March 2017, The Response of the Spokesperson of the Ministry of Foreign Affairs, Ambassador Hüseyin Müftüoğlu, to a Question Regarding the Contacts of Gkry Leader Anastasiadis with a Hydrocarbon Company in the

USA," Republic of Turkey Ministry of Foreign Affairs, accessed September 21, 2020, http://www.mfa.gov.tr/qa_18_-24-march-2017_-statement-of-the-spokesperson-of-the-ministry-of-foreign-affairs_-ambassador-h%C3%BCseyin-m%C3%BCft%C3%BCo%C4%9Flu_-in-response-to-a-question-regarding-the-contacts-of-greek-cypriot-leader-mr_-anastasiades-with-a-hydrocarbon-company-in-the-usa.en.mfa.

26. "No: 105, 6 April 2017, Regarding the signing of exploration and production contracts with some hydrocarbon companies," Republic of Turkey Ministry of Foreign Affairs, accessed September 21, 2020, http://www.mfa.gov.tr/no_-105_-6-april-2017_-press-release-regarding-the-greek-cypriot-administration_s-signing-of-exploration-and-exploitation-contracts-with-some-hydrocarbon-companies.en.mfa.

27. "No: 400, 29 December 2017, Regarding the Hydrocarbon Activities of the GASC in the Eastern Mediterranean," Republic of Turkey Ministry of Foreign Affairs, accessed September 21, 2020, http://www.mfa.gov.tr/no_-400_-gkrynin-dogu-akdenizdeki-hidrokarbon-faaliyetleri-hk_en.en.mfa.

28. "No: 43, 11 February 2018, Regarding the Hydrocarbon Activities of the GASC in the Eastern Mediterranean," Republic of Turkey Ministry of Foreign Affairs, accessed September 22, 2020, http://www.mfa.gov.tr/no_-43_-gkrynin-dogu-akdenizdeki-hidrokarbon-faaliyetleri-hk.en.mfa.

29. "QA-53, 30 July 2018, Statement of the Spokesperson of the Ministry of Foreign Affairs, Mr. Hami Aksoy, in response to a question regarding the remarks of some Ambassadors concerning the Greek Cypriot administration's unilateral hydrocarbon-related activities in the Eastern Mediterranean," Republic of Turkey Ministry of Foreign Affairs, accessed September 21, 2020, http://www.mfa.gov.tr/sc_-53_-bazi-buyukelcilerin-gkrynin-dogu-akdenizdeki-tek-tarafli-hidrokarbon-faaliyetlerine-iliskin-ifadeleri-hk-sc_en.en.mfa.

30. "No: 265, 4 October 2018, Regarding the Decision of the GASC to Invite International Companies for the So-called License Field No.7," Republic of Turkey Ministry of Foreign Affairs, accessed September 21, 2020, http://www.mfa.gov.tr/no_-265_-gkry-nin-sozde-ruhsat-sahasi-icin-uluslararasi-sirketlere-daveti-hk_en.en.mfa.

31. "No:39—1 March 2007, Press Release Regarding the Defense Cooperation Agreement; between France and the Greek Cypriot administration of Southern Cyprus," Republic of Turkey Ministry of Foreign Affairs, accessed September 21, 2020, http://www.mfa.gov.tr/_p_no_39---1-march-2007_-press-release-regarding-the-defence-cooperation-agreement_between-france-and-the-greek-cypriot-administration-of-southern-cyprus-_unofficial-translation_-__p_.en.mfa.

32. "No: 124, 4 May 2019, Press Release Regarding the Statement by the High Representative of the EU for Foreign Affairs and Security Policy, Federica Mogherini," Republic of Turkey Ministry of Foreign Affairs, accessed September 21, 2020, http://www.mfa.gov.tr/no_124_-ab-dis-iliskiler-ve-guvenlik-politikasi-ytem-silcisinin-aciklamasi-hk.en.mfa.

33. QA-41, 7 June 2019, Statement of the Spokesperson of the Ministry of Foreign Affairs, Mr. Hami Aksoy, in Response to a Question Regarding the Greek Cypriot administration's Recent Agreement on Natural Gas Revenue Sharing with Certain International Oil, Republic of Turkey Ministry of Foreign Affairs, accessed

September 21, 2020, http://www.mfa.gov.tr/sc_-41_-gkry-nin-dogu-akdenizde-bazi-petrol-sirketleri-ile-yaptigi-anlasma-hk-sc.en.mfa.

34. "No: 170, 15 June 2019, Press Release Regarding the Joint Declaration Adopted at the Sixth MED7 Summit," Republic of Turkey Ministry of Foreign Affairs, accessed September 21, 2020, http://www.mfa.gov.tr/no_170_-altinci-med7-zirvesinde-kabul-edilen-ortak-bildiri-hk.en.mfa.

35. "No: 199, 10 July 2019, Press Release Regarding the Activities of our Drilling Ship Yavuz," Republic of Turkey Ministry of Foreign Affairs, accessed September 21, 2020, http://www.mfa.gov.tr/no_199_-yavuz-sondaj-gemimizin-faaliyetleri-hk.en.mfa.

36. Republic of Turkey Ministry of Foreign Affairs, "Comply With The Proposal Or We Will Continue," accessed September 21, 2020, http://www.mfa.gov.tr/disisleri-bakani-sayin-mevlut-cavusoglu_nun-kibris-postasi-gazetesinde-yayinlanan-makalesi.en.mfa.

37. "QA-56, 19 September 2019, Statement of the Spokesperson of the Ministry of Foreign Affairs, Mr. Hami Aksoy, in Response to the Press Reports that the Greek Cypriot administration Signed Agreements with International Companies for Offshore Hydrocarbon Exploration within So-called License Area Number 7," Republic of Turkey Ministry of Foreign Affairs, accessed September 21, 2020, http://www.mfa.gov.tr/sc_-56_-sozde-ruhsat-sahasi-hk-sc.en.mfa.

38. "QA-58, 28 September 2019, Statement of the Spokesperson of the Ministry of the Foreign Affairs, Mr. Hami Aksoy, in Response to a Question Regarding the Joint Statement of the Greece-Egypt-GCA Trilateral Meeting," Republic of Turkey Ministry of Foreign Affairs, accessed September 21, 2020, http://www.mfa.gov.tr/sc_-58_-yunanistan-misir-gkry-hk-sc.en.mfa.

39. "No: 292, 9 October 2019, Press Release Regarding the Declaration Published at the End of the Egypt-Greece-GASC Summit," Republic of Turkey Ministry of Foreign Affairs, accessed September 21, 2020, http://www.mfa.gov.tr/no_292_-misir-yunanistan-gkry-zirvesi-hk.en.mfa.

40. "No: 329, 11 November 2019, Regarding the Decisions Taken by the EU External Relations Council," Republic of Turkey Ministry of Foreign Affairs, accessed September 21, 2020, http://www.mfa.gov.tr/no_329_-ab-dis-iliskiler-konseyi-nin-aldigi-kararlar-hk.en.mfa.

41. "QA-73, 1 December 2019, Statement of the Spokesperson of the Ministry of the Foreign Affairs, Mr. Hami Aksoy, in Response to a Question Regarding the Statements Made by Greece and Egypt on the Agreement Signed with Libya on the Maritime Jurisdiction Areas," Republic of Turkey Ministry of Foreign Affairs, accessed September 21, 2020, http://www.mfa.gov.tr/sc_-73_-yunanistan-ve-misir-aciklamalari-hk-sc.en.mfa.

42. We use the name "Republic of Cyprus (RoC)" adhering to the original statements of Hellenic Ministry of Foreign Affairs.

43. 6 October 2011, "Foreign Minister Lambrinidis's reply to a question in parliament from LAOS MP Velopoulos," Hellenic Republic Ministry of Foreign Affairs, accessed September 21, 2020, https://www.mfa.gr/en/current-affairs/top-story/foreign-minister-lambrinidiss-reply-to-question-in-parliament-from-laos-mp-velopoulos-october-2011.html.

44. 11 September 2012, "Statements of Foreign Minister Avramopoulos and the Foreign Minister of the Republic of Cyprus, E. Markoullis, following their meeting Tuesday," Hellenic Republic, Ministry of Foreign Affairs, accessed September 21,2020, https://www.mfa.gr/en/current-affairs/top-story/statements-of-foreign-minister-avramopoulos-and-the-foreign-minister-of-the-republic-of-cyprus-markoullis-following-their-meeting.html.

45. 14.02.2014, "Briefing of the Parliamentary Standing Committee on Defense and Foreign Affairs, by Deputy Prime Minister and Foreign Minister Evangelos Venizelos," Hellenic Republic, Ministry of Foreign Affairs, accessed September 21, 2020, https://www.mfa.gr/en/current-affairs/top-story/briefing-of-the-parliamentarystanding-committee-on-defense-and-foreign-affairs-by-deputy-prime-minister-and-foreign-ministerevangelos-venizelos.html.

46. 28 March 2016, "Foreign Ministry spokesperson Koutras' response to journalists' questions on the Turkish Foreign Ministry announcement regarding the call for the third round of tenders for licensing of exploration in the Cypriot EEZ," Hellenic Republic Ministry of Foreign Affairs, accessed September 21, 2020, https://www.mfa.gr/turkey/tr/the-embassy/news/foreign-ministry-spokesperson-koutras-response-to-journalists-questions-on-the-turkish-foreign-ministry-announcement-regarding-the-call-for-the-third-round-of-tenders-for-licensing-of-exploration-in-the-cypriot-eez.html.

47. 24 February 2018, "Interview of Minister of Foreign Affairs, Nikos Kotzias, on ERT Radio 1's 'Politika Paralipomena', with journalist Alfonsos Vitalis Saturday, Hellenic Republic Ministry of Foreign Affairs," accessed September 21, 2020, https://www.mfa.gr/en/current-affairs/top-story/interview-of-minister-of-foreign-affairs-nikos-kotzias-on-ert-radio-1s-politika-paralipomena-with-journalist-alfonsos-vitalis.html.

48. 5 March 2018, Athens, "Joint statements of the Ministers of Foreign Affairs of Greece and the Republic of Cyprus, Nikos Kotzias and Nikos Christodoulides, following their meeting," Hellenic Republic Ministry of Foreign Affairs, accessed September 21, 2020, https://www.mfa.gr/en/current-affairs/top-story/joint-statements-of-the-ministers-of-foreign-affairs-of-greece-and-the-republic-of-cyprus-nikos-kotzias-and-nikos-christodoulides-following-their-meeting-athens-march-2018.html.

49. 20.12.2018, Beersheba, "Israel-Cyprus-Greece 5th Trilateral Summit Declaration," Hellenic Republic Ministry of Foreign Affairs, accessed September 21, 2020, https://www.mfa.gr/en/current-affairs/statements-speeches/israel-cyprus-greece-5th-trilateral-summit-declaration-beersheba-december-20th-2018.html.

50. 20.12.2018, Beersheba, "Statements of Prime Minister and Minister of Foreign Affairs, Alexis Tsipras, following the proceedings of the 5th Greece-Cyprus-Israel Trilateral Summit Meeting," Hellenic Republic Ministry of Foreign Affairs, accessed September 21, 2020, https://www.mfa.gr/en/current-affairs/top-story/statements-of-prime-minister-and-minister-of-foreign-affairs-alexis-tsipras-following-the-proceedings-of-the-5th-greece-cyprus-israel-trilateral-summit-meeting-beersheba-20-december-2018.html.

51. 29 January 2019, "Nicosia, Statements by Prime Minister and Minister of Foreign Affairs, Alexis Tsipras, following the proceedings of the 5th Southern

EU Countries Summit," Hellenic Republic Ministry of Foreign Affairs, accessed September 21, 2020, https://www.mfa.gr/missionsabroad/en/malta-en/news/statements-by-prime-minister-and-minister-of-foreign-affairs-alexis-tsipras-following-the-proceedings-of-the-5th-southern-eu-countries-summit-nicosia-29-january-2019.html.

52. 5 February 2019, "Ankara, Statements by Prime Minister and Minister of Foreign Affairs Alexis Tsipras during the joint Press Conference with the President of the Republic of Turkey, Recep Tayyip Erdoğan," Hellenic Republic Ministry of Foreign Affairs, accessed September 21, 2020, https://www.mfa.gr/en/current-affairs/top-story/statements-by-prime-minister-and-minister-of-foreign-affairs-alexis-tsipras-during-the-joint-press-conference-with-the-president-of-the-republic-of-turkey-recep-tayyip-erdogan-ankara-february-2019.html.

53. 21.03.2019, Antalya, "Statements by Minister of Foreign Affairs Giorgos Katrougalos following the conclusion of his meeting with his Turkish counterpart, Mevlüt Çavuşoğlu," Hellenic Republic Ministry of Foreign Affairs, accessed September 21, 2020, https://www.mfa.gr/en/current-affairs/top-story/statements-by-minister-of-foreign-affairs-giorgos-katrougalos-following-the-conclusion-of-his-meeting-with-his-turkish-counterpart-mevlut-cavusoglu-antalya-21032019.html.

54. 05.06.2019, "Minister of Foreign Affairs Giorgos Katrougalos' interview on 'Thema Radio' with journalists B. Koutras and N. Felekis. Excerpt on foreign policy issues," Hellenic Republic Ministry of Foreign Affairs, accessed September 21, 2020, https://www.mfa.gr/en/current-affairs/statements-speeches/minister-of-foreign-affairs-giorgos-katrougalos-interview-on-thema-radio-with-journalists-koutras-and-felekis-excerpt-on-foreign-policy-issues.html.

55. 06.05.2019, "Ministry of Foreign Affairs announcement on Turkey's decision to carry out illegal drilling in the Exclusive Economic Zone of the Republic of Cyprus," Hellenic Republic Ministry of Foreign Affairs, accessed September 21, 2020, https://www.mfa.gr/en/current-affairs/statements-speeches/ministry-of-foreign-affairs-announcement-on-turkeys-decision-to-carry-out-illegal-drilling-in-the-exclusive-economic-zone-of-the-republic-of-cyprus.html.

56. 15.05.2019, "Alternate Minister of Foreign Affairs Sia Anagnostopoulou's speech to the Hellenic Parliament Plenary," Hellenic Republic Ministry of Foreign Affairs, accessed September 21, 2020, https://www.mfa.gr/en/current-affairs/statements-speeches/alternate-minister-of-foreign-affairs-sia-anagnostopoulous-speech-to-the-hellenic-parliament-plenary-1505-2019.html.

57. 22.05.2019, "Speech by the President of the Republic, Mr. Prokopis Pavlopoulos and by the Minister of Foreign Affairs, Mr. Giorgos Katrougalos, at the swearing-in ceremony of the 24th Class of Ministry of Foreign Affairs Attachés," Hellenic Republic Ministry of Foreign Affairs, accessed September 21, 2020, https://www.mfa.gr/en/current-affairs/top-story/speech-by-the-president-of-the-republic-mr-prokopis-pavlopoulos-and-by-the-minister-of-foreign-affairs-mr-giorgos-katrougalos-at-the-swearing-in-ceremony-of-the-24th-class-of-ministry-of-foreign-affairs-attaches-22-may-2019.html.

58. 06.06.2019, Athens, "Statements by the Alternate Minister of Foreign Affairs, Sia Anagnostopoulou, following her meeting with the Estonian Undersecretary for

European Affairs, Matti Maasikas," Hellenic Republic Ministry of Foreign Affairs, accessed September 21, 2020, https://www.mfa.gr/en/current-affairs/statements-speeches/statements-by-the-alternate-minister-of-foreign-affairs-sia-anagnostopoulou-following-her-meeting-with-the-estonian-undersecretary-for-european-affairs-matti-maasikas-athens-june-2019.html.

59. 14.06.2019, "Minister of Foreign Affairs Giorgos Katrougalos' interview on "Radio 9.84" (Crete), with journalist Giorgos Sachinis—Excerpts on foreign policy," Hellenic Republic Ministry of Foreign Affairs, accessed September 21, 2020, https://www.mfa.gr/en/current-affairs/statements-speeches/minister-of-foreign-affairs-giorgos-katrougalos-interview-on-radio-984-crete-with-journalist-giorgos-sachinis-excerpts-on-foreign-policy.html.

60. 18.06.2019, "Minister of Foreign Affairs Giorgos Katrougalos' article in newspaper Ta Nea," Hellenic Republic Ministry of Foreign Affairs, accessed September 21, 2020, https://www.mfa.gr/en/current-affairs/statements-speeches/minister-of-foreign-affairs-giorgos-katrougalos-article-in-newspaper-ta-nea-18-june-2019.html.

61. 21.06.2019, "Excerpts from Alternate Minister of Foreign Affairs Sia Anagnostopoulou's interview on AMNA 'Praktorio 104.9' radio, with journalists Sofia Papadopoulou and Kostas Papadakis," Hellenic Republic Ministry of Foreign Affairs, accessed September 21, 2020, https://www.mfa.gr/en/current-affairs/statements-speeches/excerpts-from-alternate-minister-of-foreign-affairs-sia-anagnostopoulous-interview-on-amna-praktorio-1049-radio-with-journalists-sofia-papadopoulou-and-kostas-papadakis-21-june-2019.html.

62. 22.06.2019, "Minister of Foreign Affairs Giorgos Katrougalos' interview in the Athens daily 'Efimerida ton Syntakton', with journalist N. Zirganos," Hellenic Republic Ministry of Foreign Affairs, accessed September 21, 2020, https://www.mfa.gr/en/current-affairs/top-story/minister-of-foreign-affairs-giorgos-katrougalos-interview-in-the-athens-daily-efimerida-ton-syntakton-with-journalist-zirganos-22-june-2019.html.

63. 23.06.2019, "Minister of Foreign Affairs Giorgos Katrougalos' interview in the Athens daily 'REAL NEWS', with journalist P. Klavdianos Sunday," Hellenic Republic Ministry of Foreign Affairs, accessed September 21, 2020, https://www.mfa.gr/en/current-affairs/statements-speeches/minister-of-foreign-affairs-giorgos-katrougalos-interview-in-the-athens-daily-real-news-with-journalist-klavdianos.html.

64. 28.06.2019, "Main points of Minister of Foreign Affairs Giorgos Katrougalos' statements on 'Newsit Debate', with journalist Nikos Evangelatos," Hellenic Republic Ministry of Foreign Affairs, accessed September 21, 2020, https://www.mfa.gr/en/current-affairs/statements-speeches/main-points-of-minister-of-foreign-affairs-giorgos-katrougalos-statements-on-newsit-debate-with-journalist-nikos-evangelatos-28-june-2019.html.

65. 30.06.2019, "Energy as a Game Changer: Article on the EastMed pipeline, in the 'Sunday Kathimerini', by Minister of Foreign Affairs Giorgos Katrougalos," Hellenic Republic Ministry of Foreign Affairs, accessed September 21, 2020, https://www.mfa.gr/en/current-affairs/statements-speeches/energy-as-game-changer-article-on-the-eastmed-pipeline-in-the-sunday-kathimerini-by-minister-of-foreign-affairs-giorgos-katrougalos.html.

66. 17.07.2019, "Minister of Foreign Affairs Nikos Dendias' interview in the New York daily 'National Herald' (Ethnikos Kirikas)," Hellenic Republic Ministry of Foreign Affairs, accessed September 21, 2020, https://www.mfa.gr/usa/en/the-embassy/news/minister-of-foreign-affairs-nikos-dendias-interview-in-the-new-york-daily-national-herald-ethnikos-kirikas-17-july-2019.html.

67. 17.07.2019, Washington," Statement of the Minister of Foreign Affairs, Nikos Dendias, to Greek correspondents following his meeting with U.S. Secretary of State, Mike Pompeo," Hellenic Republic Ministry of Foreign Affairs, accessed September 21, 2020, https://www.mfa.gr/usa/en/consulate-general-in-chicago/news/statement-of-the-minister-of-foreign-affairs-nikos-dendias-to-greek-correspondents-following-his-meeting-with-us-secretary-of-state-mike-pompeo-washington-17-july-2019.html.

68. 04.08.2019, "Alternate Minister of Foreign Affairs Miltiadis Varvitsiotis' interview in the 'Sunday Ethnos', with journalist S. Mourelatos," Hellenic Republic Ministry of Foreign Affairs, accessed September 21, 2020, https://www.mfa.gr/en/current-affairs/statements-speeches/alternate-minister-of-foreign-affairs-miltiadis-varvitsiotis-interview-in-the-sunday-ethnos-with-journalist-mourelatos-august-2019.html.

69. 31.08.2019, "Interview of Alternate Minister of Foreign Affairs Miltiadis Varvitsiotis in 'Sunday Vradyni', with journalist C. Kantas," Hellenic Republic Ministry of Foreign Affairs, accessed September 21, 2020, https://www.mfa.gr/en/current-affairs/statements-speeches/interview-of-alternate-minister-of-foreign-affairs-miltiadis-varvitsiotis-in-sunday-vradyni-with-journalist-kantas-31-august-2019.html.

70. 04.10.2019, "Interview of Minister of Foreign Affairs Nikos Dendias on 'ANT1 TV'", with journalist Nikos Hatzinikolaou," Hellenic Republic Ministry of Foreign Affairs, accessed September 21, 2020, https://www.mfa.gr/en/current-affairs/statements-speeches/interview-of-minister-of-foreign-affairs-nikos-dendias-on-ant1-tv-with-journalist-nikos-hatzinikolaou-october-2019.html.

71. 09.10.2019, "Minister of Foreign Affairs, Nikos Dendias, speaks on ERT1 TV's "Politiki Epikairotita" with reporters N. Meletis and F. Papathanasiou," Hellenic Republic Ministry of Foreign Affairs, accessed September 21, 2020, https://www.mfa.gr/en/current-affairs/top-story/minister-of-foreign-affairs-nikos-dendias-speaks-on-ert1-tvs-politiki-epikairotita-with-reporters-meletis-and-papathanasiou-october-2019.html.

72. 08.12.2019, "Interview of the Minister of Foreign Affairs, Nikos Dendias, on ANT1 TV, with journalists N. Rogakos and P. Stathis," Hellenic Republic Ministry of Foreign Affairs, accessed September 21, 2020, https://www.mfa.gr/en/current-affairs/statements-speeches/interview-of-the-minister-of-foreign-affairs-nikos-dendias-on-ant1-tv-with-journalists-rogakos-and-stathis-december-2019.html.

73. 15.12.2019, Athens, "Speech of the Minister of Foreign Affairs, Nikos Dendias, during the Hellenic Parliament's debate of the 2020 budget—References to foreign policy issues," Hellenic Republic Ministry of Foreign Affairs, accessed September 21, 2020, https://www.mfa.gr/en/current-affairs/top-story/speech-of-the-minister-of-foreign-affairs-nikos-dendias-during-the-hellenic-parliaments-debate

-of-the-2020-budget-references-to-foreign-policy-issues-athens-15-december-2019.html.

74. 22.12.2019, "Interview of the Minister of Foreign Affairs, Nikos Dendias, in the Athens daily 'Real News', with journalists P. Galatsiatos and G. Siadimas," Hellenic Republic Ministry of Foreign Affairs, accessed September 21, 2020, https://www.mfa.gr/en/current-affairs/statements-speeches/interview-of-the-minister-of-foreign-affairs-nikos-dendias-in-the-athens-daily-real-news-with-journalists-galatsiatos-and-siadimas-22-december-2019.html.

REFERENCES

Hellenic Republic Ministry of Foreign Affairs. "Interview of Alternate Minister of Foreign Affairs Miltiadis Varvitsiotis in 'Sunday Vradyni', with journalist C. Kantas." Accessed September 21, 2020. https://www.mfa.gr/en/current-affairs/statements-speeches/interview-of-alternate-minister-of-foreign-affairs-miltiadis-varvitsiotis-in-sunday-vradyni-with-journalist-kantas-31-august-2019.html.

Hellenic Republic Ministry of Foreign Affairs. "Statements by the Alternate Minister of Foreign Affairs, Sia Anagnostopoulou, following her meeting with the Estonian Undersecretary for European Affairs, Matti Maasikas." Accessed September 21, 2020. https://www.mfa.gr/en/current-affairs/statements-speeches/statements-by-the-alternate-minister-of-foreign-affairs-sia-anagnostopoulou-following-her-meeting-with-the-estonian-undersecretary-for-european-affairs-matti-maasikas-athens-june-2019.html.

Hellenic Republic Ministry of Foreign Affairs. "Foreign Minister Lambrinidis's reply to a question in parliament from LAOS MP Velopoulos." Accessed September 21, 2020. ://www.mfa.gr/en/current-affairs/top-story/foreign-minister-lambrinidiss-reply-to-question-in-parliament-from-laos-mp-velopoulos-october-2011.html.

Hellenic Republic Ministry of Foreign Affairs. "Statements of Foreign Minister Avramapoulos and the Foreign Minister of the Republic of Cyprus, E. Markoullis following their meeting Tuesday." Accessed September 21, 2020. https://www.mfa.gr/en/current-affairs/top-story/statements-of-foreign-minister-avramopoulos-and-the-foreign-minister-of-the-republic-of-cyprus-markoullis-following-their-meeting.html.

Hellenic Republic Ministry of Foreign Affairs. "Briefing of the Parliamentary Standing Committee on Defense and Foreign Affairs, By Deputy Prime Minister and Foreign Minister Evangelos Venizelos." Accessed September 21, 2020. https://www.mfa.gr/en/current-affairs/top-story/briefing-of-the-parliamentarystanding-committee-on-defense-and-foreign-affairs-by-deputy-prime-minister-and-foreign-ministerevangelos-venizelos.html.

Hellenic Republic Ministry of Foreign Affairs. "Foreign Ministry spokesperson Koutras, response to Journalists' Questions on the Turkish Foreign Ministry announcement regarding the call for the third round of tenders for licensing of exploration in the Cypriot EEZ." Accessed September 21, 2020. https://www.mfa.gr/turkey/tr/the-embassy/news/foreign-ministry-spokesperson-koutras-response

-to-journalists-questions-on-the-turkish-foreign-ministry-announcement-regarding-the-call-for-the-third-round-of-tenders-for-licensing-of-exploration-in-the-cyprio.

Hellenic Republic Ministry of Foreign Affairs. "Interview of Minister of Foreign Affairs, Nikos Kotzias on ERT Radio 1's 'Politika Paralipomena' with Journalist Alfonsos Vitalis Saturday." Accessed September 21, 2020. https://www.mfa.gr/en/current-affairs/top-story/interview-of-minister-of-foreign-affairs-nikos-kotzias-on-ert-radio-1s-politika-paralipomena-with-journalist-alfonsos-vitalis.html adresinden alındı.

Hellenic Republic Ministry of Foreign Affairs. "Israel–Cyprus–Greece 5th Triklateral Summit Declaration." Accessed September 21, 2020. https://www.mfa.gr/en/current-affairs/statements-speeches/israel-cyprus-greece-5th-trilateral-summit-declaration-beersheba-december-20th-2018.html.

Hellenic Republic Ministry of Foreign Affairs. "Joint statements of the Ministers of Foreign Affairs of Greece and the Republic of Cyprus, Nikos Kotzias and Nikos Christodoulides, following their meeting." Accessed September 21, 2020. https://www.mfa.gr/en/current-affairs/top-story/joint-statements-of-the-ministers-of-foreign-affairs-of-greece-and-the-republic-of-cyprus-nikos-kotzias-and-nikos-christodoulides-following-their-meeting-athens-march-2018.html.

Hellenic Republic Ministry of Foreign Affairs. "Statements of Prime Minister and Minister of Foreign Affairs, Alexis Tsipras, following the proceedings of the 5th Greece–Cyprus–Israel Trilateral Summit Meeting." Accessed September 21, 2020. https://www.mfa.gr/en/current-affairs/top-story/statements-of-prime-minister-and-minister-of-foreign-affairs-alexis-tsipras-following-the-proceedings-of-the-5th-greece-cyprus-israel-trilateral-summit-meeting-beersheba-20-december-2018.html.

Hellenic Republic Ministry of foreign Affairs. "Alternate Minister of Foreign Affairs Miltiadis Varvitsiotis' interview in the 'Sunday Ethnos', with journalist S. Mourelatos." Accessed September 21, 2020. https://www.mfa.gr/en/current-affairs/statements-speeches/alternate-minister-of-foreign-affairs-miltiadis-varvitsiotis-interview-in-the-sunday-ethnos-with-journalist-mourelatos-august-2019.html.

Hellenic Republic Ministry of Foreign Affairs. "Alternate Minister of Foreign Affairs Sia Anagnostopoulou's speech to the Hellenic Parliament Plenary." Accessed September 21, 2020. https://www.mfa.gr/en/current-affairs/statements-speeches/alternate-minister-of-foreign-affairs-sia-anagnostopoulous-speech-to-the-hellenic-parliament-plenary-1505-2019.html.

Hellenic Republic Ministry of Foreign Affairs. "ENERGY AS A GAME CHANGER: Article on the EastMed pipeline, in the 'Sunday Kathimerini', by Minister of Foreign Affairs Giorgos Katrougalos." Accessed September 21, 2020. https://www.mfa.gr/en/current-affairs/statements-speeches/energy-as-game-changer-article-on-the-eastmed-pipeline-in-the-sunday-kathimerini-by-minister-of-foreign-affairs-giorgos-katrougalos.html.

Hellenic Republic Ministry of Foreign Affairs. "Excerpts from Alternate Minister of Foreign Affairs Sia Anagnostopoulou's interview on AMNA 'Praktorio 104.9' radio, with journalists Sofia Papadopoulou and Kostas Papadakis." Accessed September 21, 2020. https://www.mfa.gr/en/current-affairs/statements-speeches

/excerpts-from-alternate-minister-of-foreign-affairs-sia-anagnostopoulous-interview-on-amna-praktorio-1049-radio-with-journalists-sofia-papadopoulou-and-kostas-papadakis-21-june-2019.html.

Hellenic Republic Ministry of Foreign Affairs. "Interview of Minister of Foreign Affairs Nikos Dendias on 'ANT1 TV', with journalist Nikos Hatzinikolaou." Accessed September 21, 2020. https://www.mfa.gr/en/current-affairs/statements-speeches/interview-of-minister-of-foreign-affairs-nikos-dendias-on-ant1-tv-with-journalist-nikos-hatzinikolaou-october-2019.html.

Hellenic Republic Ministry of Foreign Affairs. "Interview of the Minister of Foreign Affairs, Nikos Dendias, in the Athens daily 'Real News', with journalists P. Galatsiatos and G. Siadimas." Accessed September 21, 2020. https://www.mfa.gr/en/current-affairs/statements-speeches/interview-of-the-minister-of-foreign-affairs-nikos-dendias-in-the-athens-daily-real-news-with-journalists-galatsiatos-and-siadimas-22-december-2019.html.

Hellenic Republic Ministry of Foreign Affairs. "Interview of the Minister of Foreign Affairs, Nikos Dendias, on ANT1 TV, with journalists N. Rogakos and P. Stathis." Accessed September 21, 2020. https://www.mfa.gr/en/current-affairs/statements-speeches/interview-of-the-minister-of-foreign-affairs-nikos-dendias-on-ant1-tv-with-journalists-rogakos-and-stathis-december-2019.html.

Hellenic Republic Ministry of Foreign Affairs. "Main points of Minister of Foreign Affairs Giorgos Katrougalos' statements on 'Newsit Debate", with journalist Nikos Evangelatos." Retrieved from Accessed September 21, 2020. https://www.mfa.gr/en/current-affairs/statements-speeches/main-points-of-minister-of-foreign-affairs-giorgos-katrougalos-statements-on-newsit-debate-with-journalist-nikos-evangelatos-28-june-2019.html.

Hellenic Republic Ministry of Foreign Affairs. "Minister of Foreign Affairs Giorgos Katrougalos' article in newspaper Ta Nea." Accessed September 21, 2020. https://www.mfa.gr/en/current-affairs/statements-speeches/minister-of-foreign-affairs-giorgos-katrougalos-article-in-newspaper-ta-nea-18-june-2019.html.

Hellenic Republic Ministry of Foreign Affairs. "Minister of Foreign Affairs Giorgos Katrougalos' interview in the Athens daily 'REAL NEWS', with journalist P. Klavdianos." Accessed September 21, 2020. https://www.mfa.gr/en/current-affairs/statements-speeches/minister-of-foreign-affairs-giorgos-katrougalos-interview-in-the-athens-daily-real-news-with-journalist-klavdianos.html.

Hellenic Republic Ministry of Foreign Affairs. "Minister of Foreign Affairs Giorgos Katrougalos' interview on 'Thema Radio' with journalists B. Koutras and N. Felekis. Excerpt on foreign policy issues." Accessed September 21, 2020. https://www.mfa.gr/en/current-affairs/statements-speeches/minister-of-foreign-affairs-giorgos-katrougalos-interview-on-thema-radio-with-journalists-koutras-and-felekis-excerpt-on-foreign-policy-issues.html.

Hellenic Republic Ministry of foreign Affairs. "Minister of Foreign Affairs Giorgos Katrougalos' interview on "Radio 9.84" (Crete), with journalist Giorgos Sachinis—Excerpts on foreign policy." Accessed September 21, 2020. https://www.mfa.gr/en/current-affairs/statements-speeches/minister-of-foreign-affairs

-giorgos-katrougalos-interview-on-radio-984-crete-with-journalist-giorgos-sachinis-excerpts-on-foreign-policy.html.

Hellenic Republic Ministry of Foreign Affairs. "Minister of Foreign Affairs Nikos Dendias' interview in the New York daily 'National Herald' (Ethnikos Kirikas)." Accessed September 21, 2020. https://www.mfa.gr/usa/en/the-embassy/news/minister-of-foreign-affairs-nikos-dendias-interview-in-the-new-york-daily-national-herald-ethnikos-kirikas-17-july-2019.html.

Hellenic Republic Ministry of Foreign Affairs. "Minister of Foreign Affairs, Nikos Dendias, speaks on ERT1 TV's "Politiki Epikairotita" with reporters N. Meletis and F. Papathanasiou." Retrieved from Accessed September 21, 2020. https://www.mfa.gr/en/current-affairs/top-story/minister-of-foreign-affairs-nikos-dendias-speaks-on-ert1-tvs-politiki-epikairotita-with-reporters-meletis-and-papathanasiou-october-2019.html.

Hellenic Republic Ministry of Foreign Affairs. "Ministry of Foreign Affairs announcement on Turkey's decision to carry out illegal drilling in the Exclusive Economic Zone of the Republic of Cyprus." Accessed September 21, 2020. https://www.mfa.gr/en/current-affairs/statements-speeches/ministry-of-foreign-affairs-announcement-on-turkeys-decision-to-carry-out-illegal-drilling-in-the-exclusive-economic-zone-of-the-republic-of-cyprus.html.

Hellenic Republic Ministry of Foreign Affairs. "Speech by the President of the Republic, Mr. Prokopis Pavlopoulos and by the Minister of Foreign Affairs, Mr Giorgos Katrougalos, at the swearing-in ceremony of the 24th Class of Ministry of Foreign Affairs Attachés." Accessed September 21, 2020. https://www.mfa.gr/en/current-affairs/top-story/speech-by-the-president-of-the-republic-mr-prokopis-pavlopoulos-and-by-the-minister-of-foreign-affairs-mr-giorgos-katrougalos-at-the-swearing-in-ceremony-of-the-24th-class-of-ministry-of-foreign-affairs-atta.

Hellenic Republic Ministry of Foreign Affairs. "Speech of the Minister of Foreign Affairs, Nikos Dendias, during the Hellenic Parliament's debate of the 2020 budget—References to foreign policy issues." Accessed September 21, 2020. https://www.mfa.gr/en/current-affairs/top-story/speech-of-the-minister-of-foreign-affairs-nikos-dendias-during-the-hellenic-parliaments-debate-of-the-2020-budget-references-to-foreign-policy-issues-athens-15-december-2019.html.

Hellenic Republic Ministry of Foreign Affairs. "Statement of the Minister of Foreign Affairs, Nikos Dendias, to Greek correspondents following his meeting with U.S. Secretary of State, Mike Pompeo." Accessed September 21, 2020. https://www.mfa.gr/usa/en/consulate-general-in-chicago/news/statement-of-the-minister-of-foreign-affairs-nikos-dendias-to-greek-correspondents-following-his-meeting-with-us-secretary-of-state-mike-pompeo-washington-17-july-2019.html.

Hellenic Republic Ministry of Foreign Affairs. "Statements by Minister of Foreign Affairs Giorgos Katrougalos following the conclusion of his meeting with his Turkish counterpart, Mevlüt Çavuşoğlu." Accessed September 21, 2020. https://www.mfa.gr/en/current-affairs/top-story/statements-by-minister-of-foreign-affairs-giorgos-katrougalos-following-the-conclusion-of-his-meeting-with-his-turkish-counterpart-mevlut-cavusoglu-antalya-21032019.html.

Hellenic Republic Ministry of Foreign Affairs. "Statements by Prime Minister and Minister of Foreign Affairs Alexis Tsipras during the joint Press Conference with the President of the Republic of Turkey, Recep Tayyip Erdoğan." Accessed September 21, 2020. https://www.mfa.gr/en/current-affairs/top-story/statements-by-prime-minister-and-minister-of-foreign-affairs-alexis-tsipras-during-the-joint-press-conference-with-the-president-of-the-republic-of-turkey-recep-tayyip-erdogan-ankara-february-2019.html.

Hellenic Republic Ministry of Foreign Affairs. "Statements by Prime Minister and Minister of Foreign Affairs, Alexis Tsipras, following the proceedings of the 5th Southern EU Countries Summi." Accessed 21, 2020. https://www.mfa.gr/missionsabroad/en/malta-en/news/statements-by-prime-minister-and-minister-of-foreign-affairs-alexis-tsipras-following-the-proceedings-of-the-5th-southern-eu-countries-summit-nicosia-29-january-2019.html.

Hellenic Republic Ministry of Foreign Affairs. "Minister of Foreign Affairs Giorgos Katrougalos' interview in the Athens daily 'Efimerida ton Syntakton', with journalist N. Zirganos." Accessed September 21, 2020. https://www.mfa.gr/en/current-affairs/top-story/minister-of-foreign-affairs-giorgos-katrougalos-interview-in-the-athens-daily-efimerida-ton-syntakton-with-journalist-zirganos-22-june-2019.html.

İşeri Emre "Turkey's Entangled (Energy) Security Concerns and the Cyprus Question in the Eastern Mediterranean." In Greece and Turkey in Conflict and Cooperation: From Europeanization to De-Europeanization, edited by Alexis Heraclides, Gizem Alioğlu Çakmak, 257–70. NewYork: Routledge, 2019.

İşeri Emre, Andrikopoulos Panagiotis, "Energy Geopolitics of the Eastern Mediterranean: Will Aphrodite's Lure Fuel Peace in Cyprus?," Middle Eastern Analysis 5, no. 51 (2013): 38.

Linguistic Society of America. "Discourse Analysis—What Speakers Do in Conversation." Accessed September 22, 2020. https://www.linguisticsociety.org/resource/discourse-analysis-what-speakers-do-conversation.

Lesser, Ian. "Eastern Mediterranean Brinkmanship Is a Clear and Present Danger," The German Marshall Fund of the United States, August 28, 2020, https://www.gmfus.org/blog/2020/08/28/eastern-mediterranean-brinkmanship-clear-and-present-danger#utm_source=Twitter&utm_medium=Social.

Republic of Turkey Ministry of Foreign Affairs. "QA-18 The Response of the kesperson of the Ministry of Foreign Affairs, Ambassador Hüseyin Müftüoğlu to a Question Regarding the Contacs of GKRY Leader Anastasiadis with a Hydrocarbon Company in the USA." Accessed September 21, 2020. http://www.mfa.gov.tr/qa_18_-24-march-2017_-statement-of-the-spokesperson-of-the-ministry-of-foreign-affairs_-ambassador-h%C3%BCseyin-m%C3%BCft%C3%BCo%C4%9Flu_-in-response-to-a-question-regarding-the-contacts-of-greek-cypriot-leader-mr_-anastasiades-with-.

Republic of Turkey Ministry of Foreign Affairs. "QA-56 Statement of the Spokeperson of the Ministry of Foreign Affairs, Mr. Hami Aksoy, in Response to the Press Reports that the Greek Cypriot administration Signed Agreements with International Companies for Off-shore Hydrocarbon Exploration." Accessed

September 21, 2020. http://www.mfa.gov.tr/sc_-56_-sozde-ruhsat-sahasi-hk-sc.en.mfa.

Republic of Turkey Ministry of Foreign Affairs. "Regarding the Drilling Activities of GASC." Accessed September 21, 2020. http://www.mfa.gov.tr/no_-311_-04-october-2014_-press-release-regarding-drilling-activity-of-the-greek-cypriots.en.mfa.

Republic of Turkey Ministry of Foreign Affairs. "No-39 Press Relase Regarding the Defense Cooperation Agreement; between France and the Greek Cypriot administration of Southern Cyprus." Accessed September 21, 2020. http://www.mfa.gov.tr/_p_no_39---1-march-2007_-press-release-regarding-the-defence-cooperation-agreement_between-france-and-the-greek-cypriot-administration-of-southern-cyprus-_unofficial-translation_-__p_.en.mfa.

Republic of Turkey Ministry of Foreign Affairs. "Press Release Regarding the efforts of the Greek Cypriot administration of Southern Cyprus to sign bilateral agreements concerning maritime jurisdiction areas with the countries in the Eastern Mediterranean." Accessed September 21, 2020. http://www.mfa.gov.tr/_p_30-january-2007_-press-release-regarding-the-efforts-of-the-greek-cypriot-administration-of-southern-cyprus-to-sign-bilateral-agreements-concerning-maritime-jurisdiction-areas-with-the-countries-in-the-eastern-mediterranean_br___p.

Republic of Turkey Ministry of Foreign Affairs. "Statement of the Spokesman of the Ministry of Foreign Affairs of Turkey in Response to a Question." Accessed September 21, 2020. http://www.mfa.gov.tr/_p_qa_32---statement-of-the-spokesman-of-the-ministry-of-foreign-affairs-of-turkey-in-response-to-a-question-_unofficial-translation___p_.en.mfa.

Republic of Turkey Ministry of Foreign Affairs. "The answer of The Ministry of Foreign Affair's Spokesperson to a Question." Accessed September 21, 2020. http://www.mfa.gov.tr/qa_20_-28-july-2009_-statement-of-the-spokesman-of-the-ministry-of-foreign-affairs-of-turkey-in-response-to-a-question.en.mfa.

Republic of Turkey Ministry of Foreign Affairs. "Regarding the EEZ Agreement Signed between GCASC and Israel." Accessed September 21, 2020. http://www.mfa.gov.tr/no_-288_-21-december-2010_-press-release-regarding-the-exclusive-economic-zone-_eez_-delimitation-agreement--signed-between-greek-cypriot-administration-and-israel.en.mfa.

Republic of Turkey Ministry of Foreign Affairs. "Regarding the GCASC's Oil and Gas Exploration Activities in the Eastern Mediterranean." Accessed September 21, 2020. http://www.mfa.gov.tr/no_-181_-5-august-2011_-press-release-regarding-the-greek-cypriot-administration_s-gas-exploration-activities-in-the-eastern-mediterranean.en.mfa.

Republic of Turkey Ministry of Foreign Affairs. "TRNC Press Statement Regarding Signing of TRNC Continental Shelf Limitation Agreement of Ministry of Foreign Affairs." Accessed September 21, 2020. http://www.mfa.gov.tr/no_-216_-21-september-2011_-press-statement-on-the-continental-shelf-delimitation-agreement-signed-between-turkey-and-the-trnc.en.mfa.

Republic of Turkey Ministry of Foreign Affairs. "TRNC Press Statement Regarding Signing of TRNC Continental Shelf Limitation Agreement of Ministry of Foreign Affairs." Accessed September 21, 2020. http://www.mfa.gov.tr/no_-216_-21

-september-2011_-press-statement-on-the-continental-shelf-delimitation-agreement-signed-between-turkey-and-the-trnc.en.mfa.

Republic of Turkey Ministry of Foreign Affairs. "Regarding the Second International Hydrocarbon Exploration Tender Opened by the GCASC." Accessed September 21, 2020. http://www.mfa.gov.tr/no_-140_-18-may-2012_-press-release-regarding-the-international-tender-for-off_shore-hydrocarbon-exploration-and-exploitation-opened-by-the-greek-cypriot-administration.en.mfa.

Republic of Turkey Ministry of Foreign Affairs. "Second International Hydrocarbon Exploration Tender Opened by Southern Cyprus." Accessed September 21, 2020. http://www.mfa.gov.tr/no_-43_-15-february-2012_-second-international-tender-for-off_shore-hydrocarbon-exploration-called-by-the-greek-cypriot-administration-_gca_.en.mfa.

Republic of Turkey Ministry of Foreign Affairs. "Regarding Declaration of Greece to the United Nations." Accessed September 21, 2020. http://www.mfa.gov.tr/no_-46_-22-february-2013_-press-release-regarding-the-declaration-of-greece-to-the-united-nations.en.mfa.

Republic of Turkey Ministry of Foreign Affairs. "Regarding the Claims of GCASC on Hydrocarbon Resources in the Eastern Mediterranean." Accessed September 21, 2020. http://www.mfa.gov.tr/no_-83_-23-march-2013_-statement-regarding-the-claims-of-the-gcasc-on-hydrocarbon-resources-in-the-eastern-mediterranean.en.mfa.

Republic of Turkey Ministry of Foreign Affairs. "Prime Minister Davutoglu met with the TRNC Prime Minister." Accessed September 21, 2020. http://www.mfa.gov.tr/prime-minister-davutoglu-met-with-the-prime-minister-of-trnc.en.mfa.

Republic of Turkey Ministry of Foreign Affairs. "Regarding the Decision of the Greek Cypriot Party not to Participate in the Negotiations in the UN Negotiations Process." Accessed September 21, 2020. http://www.mfa.gov.tr/no_-313_-08-october-2014_-press-release-regarding-the-decision-of-the-greek-cypriot-administration-not-to-participate-in-the-discussions-of-the-un-negotiation-process.en.mfa.

Republic of Turkey Ministry of Foreign Affairs. "Regarding the Third International Hydrocarbon Exploration Tender Opened by the GASC." Accessed September 21, 2020. http://www.mfa.gov.tr/no_-74_-25-march-2016_-press-release-regarding-the-third-international-tender-for-off_shore-hydrocarbon-exploration-by-the-greek-cypriot-administration.en.mfa.

Republic of Turkey Ministry of Foreign Affairs. "No: 400 Regarding the Hydrocarbon Activities of the GASC in the Eastern Mediterranean." Accessed September 21, 2020. http://www.mfa.gov.tr/no_-400_-gkrynin-dogu-akdenizdeki-hidrokarbon-faaliyetleri-hk_en.en.mfa.

Republic of Turkey Ministry of Foreign Affairs. "Regarding the signing of exploration and production contracts with some hydrocarbon companies." Accessed September 21, 2020. http://www.mfa.gov.tr/no_-105_-6-april-2017_-press-release-regarding-the-greek-cypriot-administration_s-signing-of-exploration-and-exploitation-contracts-with-some-hydrocarbon-companies.en.mfa.

Republic of Turkey Ministry of Foreign Affairs. "No:265 Regarding the Decision of the GASC to Invite International Companies for the So-called Licence Field No:7."

Accessed September 21, 2020. http://www.mfa.gov.tr/no_-265_-gkry-nin-sozde-ruhsat-sahasi-icin-uluslararasi-sirketlere-daveti-hk_en.en.mfa.
Republic of Turkey Ministry of Foreign Affairs. "No:43 Regarding the Hydrocarbon Activities of the GASC in the Eastern Mediterranean." Accessed September 21, 2020. http://www.mfa.gov.tr/no_-43_-gkrynin-dogu-akdenizdeki-hidrokarbon-faa-liyetleri-hk.en.mfa.
Republic of Turkey Ministry of Foreign Affairs. "QA-53 Statements of the Spokesperson of the Ministry of Foreign Affairs, Mr. Hami Aksoy, in response to a question regarding the remarks of some Ambassadors concerning the Greek Cypriot administration's unilateral Hydrocarbon-related activities in the E.M." Accessed September 21, 2020. http://www.mfa.gov.tr/sc_-53_-bazi-buyukelcilerin-gkrynin-dogu-akdenizdeki-tek-tarafli-hidrokarbon-faaliyetlerine-iliskin-ifadeleri-hk-sc_en.en.mfa.
Republic of Turkey Ministry of Foreign Affairs. "No:124 Press Release Regarding the Statement by the High Representative of the EU for Foreign Affairs and Security Policy, Federica Mogherini." Accessed September 21, 2020. http://www.mfa.gov.tr/no_124_-ab-dis-iliskiler-ve-guvenlik-politikasi-ytemsilcisinin-aciklamasi-hk.en.mfa.
Republic of Turkey Ministry of Foreign Affairs, "Comply With The Proposal Or We Will Continue", Accessed September 21, 2020, http://www.mfa.gov.tr/dis-isleri-bakani-sayin-mevlut-cavusoglu_nun-kibris-postasi-gazetesinde-yayinlanan-makalesi.en.mfa.
Republic of Turkey Ministry of Foreign Affairs. "No:292 Press Release Regarding the Declaration Published at the End of the Egypr-Greece-GASC Summit." Accessed September 21, 2020. http://www.mfa.gov.tr/no_292_-misir-yunanistan-gkry-zirvesi-hk.en.mfa.
Republic of Turkey Ministry of Foreign Affairs. "No:329 Regarding the Decisions Taken by the EU External Relations Council." Accessed September 21, 2020. http://www.mfa.gov.tr/no_329_-ab-dis-iliskiler-konseyi-nin-aldigi-kararlar-hk.en.mfa.
Republic of Turkey Ministry of Foreign Affairs. "No-170 Press Release Regarding the Koint Declaration Adopted at the Sixth MED7 Summit." Accessed September 21, 2020. http://www.mfa.gov.tr/no_170_-altinci-med7-zirvesinde-kabul-edilen-ortak-bildiri-hk.en.mfa.
Republic of Turkey Ministry of Foreign Affairs. "Press Release Regarding the Activities of our Drilling Ship Yavuz." Accessed September 21, 2020. http://www.mfa.gov.tr/no_199_-yavuz-sondaj-gemimizin-faaliyetleri-hk.en.mfa.
Republic of Turkey Ministry of Foreign Affairs. "QA-41 Statement of the Spokesperson of the Ministry of Foreign Affairs, Mr. Hami Aksoy, in Response to a Question Regarding the Greek Cypriot administration's Recent Agreement on Natural Gas Revenue Sharing with Certain International Oil." Accessed September 21, 2020. http://www.mfa.gov.tr/sc_-41_-gkry-nin-dogu-akdenizde-bazi-petrol-sirketleri-ile-yaptigi-anlasma-hk-sc.en.mfa.
Republic of Turkey Ministry of Foreign Affairs. "QA-73 Statement of the Spokesperson of the Ministry of Foreign Affairs, Mr. Hami Aksoy, in Response to a Question

Regarding the Statements Made by Greece and Egypt on the Agreement Signed With Libya on the Maritime Jurisdiction Areas." Accessed September 21, 2020. http://www.mfa.gov.tr/sc_-73_-yunanistan-ve-misir-aciklamalari-hk-sc.en.mfa.

Republic of Turkey Ministry of Foreign Affairs. "Statement of the Spokesperson of the Ministry of the Foreign Affairs, Mr. Aksoy, in Response to a Question Regarding the Joint statement of the Greece-Egypt-GCA Trilateral Meeting." Accessed September 21, 2020. http://www.mfa.gov.tr/sc_-58_-yunanistan-misir-gkry-hk-sc.en.mfa.

Tanchum, Michael. "How Did the Eastern Mediterranean Become the Eye of a Geopolitical Storm?," Foreign Policy, August 20, 2020, https://foreignpolicy.com/2020/08/18/eastern-mediterranean-greece-turkey-warship-geopolitical-showdown/.

Türkeş-Kılıç, Selin. "Accessing the Rapprochement in its Second Decade: A Critical Approach to the Official Discourse between Turkey and Greece." In Greece and Turkey in Conflict and Cooperation: From Europeanization to De-Europeanization, edited by Alexis Heraclides, Gizem Alioğlu Çakmak, 181–93. New York: Routledge, 2019.

Ünlühisarcıklı, Özgür. "Turkey Disrupts What It Perceives as Maximalist Greek Policy," The German Marshall Fund of the United States, August 28, 2020, https://www.gmfus.org/blog/2020/08/28/eastern-mediterranean-brinkmanship-clear-and-present-danger#utm_source=Twitter&utm_medium=Social).

Chapter 6

Friends or Foes?

Climate and Energy Policies in Turkey

Barış Gençer Baykan

ABSTRACT

Climate change is one of the biggest problems humanity is facing. Turkey, being a part of the southern belt of Mediterranean Europe, is highly vulnerable to environmental and socio-economic consequences of climate change. Although its historical contribution to global greenhouse gas emissions (GHGs) is around 1%, Turkey is the world's twentieth largest emitter, and emissions have been doubled between 1990 and 2013. Demand for energy has been increasing due to economic and population growth. Climate change, to a larger extent, is an energy problem as burning fossil fuels like coal, oil, and gas leads to increased concentration of carbon dioxide in the atmosphere. Turkey's total primary energy supply is comprised mainly of fossil fuels with 90%, with gas accounting for 32%, coal for 30%, and oil for 27%. Recently there have been some efforts to increase the share of renewable energy sources and add the nuclear power to the energy mix. This chapter seeks to address to what extent climate and energy policies are consistent by assessing the national climate and energy strategies and roadmaps including the commitments under global climate regime. This chapter is organized as follows. First we provide a brief overview of energy policies. We then discuss the evolution of climate policies. Finally we offer brief concluding remarks on the energy and climate nexus.

Keywords: Climate Policy, Climate Change, Climate-Energy Nexus, Carbon Economy

A DEVELOPING CARBON ECONOMY

Energy issues have been central to economic, social, and political debates in the 2000s. Turkey has been keeping up with the changes in the world energy market, its regional implications, and national demand and investments. Bayraktar (2018) argues that the major challenges for Turkish energy markets are twofold. The first one is growing demand. According to the IEA (2020), Turkey will likely see the fastest medium to long-term growth in the field of energy among IEA member countries. The second challenge in the market is the dependency on imports. Energy import dependency was 51.2% in 1990; it rose to 72.4% in 2008 (TMMOB, 2020). In order to meet energy requirements, investments are being made in fossil fuel instead of renewable energy resources, protected areas are being opened up, and the environmental impact assessment (EIA) procedures are being bypassed. While achievements in the field of environmental protection are being undermined, efforts are being made to exempt from judicial supervision the projects that will inflict serious environmental damage. Administrative and legal tools of the development policy, such as the administrative framework for nuclear power plants, hyrdoelectric power plants, and stay on execution and EIA exemption, is not eco-friendly. On the other hand, policies on climate change are also being put off due to concerns that they will hamper development (Aktar and Baykan, 2012).

According to the Turkish Electricity Transmission Corporation (TEIAŞ in Turkish), the total installed power in June 2020 is 92,097 MW. The share of natural gas is 25,595 MW; 21,265 MW comes from hydropower plants; 10,097 MW from lignite; 8,967 MW from imported coal; 7,888 MW from run-of-the-river hydroelectric plants; 7,877 from wind power plants; 6,167 from solar power plants; 1,515 MW from geothermal power plants; 832 MW from biomass power plants; 811 MW hard coal power plants; 405 MW from asphaltite power plants; 364 MW from waste heat power plants; and finally 306 MW from fuel oil power plants (TENVA, 2020). Turkey's reliance on natural gas use has grown along with rising oil and gas imports, leaving the Turkish economy increasingly exposed to the volatility in oil and gas prices (IEA, 2020; Erensü, 2018). The private sector's involvement in the Turkish energy industry is a relatively new phenomenon; privatization of the industry was finalized throughout the 2000s under successive JDP (Justice and Development Party) governments. Since then, energy has been a reliable destination for the accumulation of capital. The industry witnessed some USD 50 billion in investment between 2008 and 2015, privatization of state-owned electricity distribution companies generated over USD 10 billion.

UNSUSTAINABLE ENERGY POLICY

Turkey is ranked fourth globally regarding the construction of new coal-fired power plants after China, India, and Russia. There are already twenty-five coal-fired power plants in use and three new ones under construction; more than seventy new coal-fired power plants with a total installed capacity of 66.5 GWs are currently being planned. Estimates show that these planned power plants will emit nearly 400 million tons of GHGs annually (IPC, 2016). Local coal and imported coal are the largest sources of GHG emissions. Pamir (2017: 482) argues that national coal (except hard coal) is low-grade fuel and its sulfur ratio is high, and until recently the impact of several coal-fired power plants on the ecosystem and human health has not been considered thoroughly. Health and Environment Alliance (HEAL, 2014) estimated that air pollution from the nineteen coal-fired power plants that were in operation in 2012 caused health costs of up to 3.6 billion euro per year. As the first-ever economic assessment of the health costs associated with air pollution, this study calculated that plants cause 2,876 premature deaths, 3,823 new cases of chronic bronchitis in adults, 4,311 hospital admissions, and 637,643 lost working days each year. Hydropower, considered as renewable energy, may also be harmful to biodiversity, communities, and agriculture. The hydropower development program has provoked vast local opposition, mainly in the Black Sea region (see Aksu et al., 2016; Hamsici, 2010; Eren, 2017). Kaygusuz and Arsel (2005) argue that there are two factors critical to sustainable energy development in Turkey. The first one is the energy intensity of the economy, and the second one is the decision on the mix of energy production technologies (nuclear, thermic, renewable, etc.) and primary resources (uranium, oil, wind, etc.). According to the projections of the Ministry of Energy and Natural Resources (2014), Turkey plans to have an electricity generation mix in which the share of renewable energy accounts for 30% of overall need as well as having 10% of the requirements of the transportation sector met by renewable energy by 2023. On the other hand, there is also a commitment to reduce by at least 20% (based on 2008 figures) the amount of energy consumed per unit GDP in the year 2023. Since 2011, a feed-in-tariff program Renewable Energy Support Mechanism (YEKDEM) has been in effect, offering a feed-in tariff of $0.073 per kilowatt-hour (kWh) for wind and hydropower projects, $0.105 for geothermal facilities, and $0.133 for solar energy and geothermal biomass plants. YEKDEM is extended to 30 June 2021.

FIGHTING SHY OF CLIMATE

According to the Fourth Assessment Report of the IPCC (Intergovernmental Panel on Climate Change), future climate change could critically undermine efforts for sustainable development throughout the world and especially in the Mediterranean Basin. Turkey is located in the eastern Mediterranean region, where countries are in the highest risk group (Pachauri and

Reisinger, 2007). Turkey needs to adapt to the adverse impacts of climate change.

In 1992, the United Nations Framework Convention on Climate Change (UNFCCC) was adopted and all OECD members (including Turkey) were included in the industrialized countries as Annex I and Annex II countries. Turkey asked for an exception arguing that its relative underdevelopment from other OECD member requires special treatment. This exception granted at the 7th COP (Conference of Parties) held in Marrakech/Morocco in 2001, and Turkey was removed from Annex II and added in Annex I, giving it responsibilities similar to "economies in transition" of Eastern Europe (Kaygusuz and Arsel, 2005). So Turkey did not have to commit any target for stabilizing its GHG emissions. The contours of Turkey's climate policy have remained almost intact over the past two decades. Being an Annex I party without any mitigation commitments, Turkey maintains a peculiar position under UNFCCC. Turkey became the 185th party to the Kyoto Protocol in August 2009 without undertaking any emission reduction commitment. Subsequent to twelve years of delay in signing both the Framework Convention and the Kyoto Protocol, Turkey had the highest rate of increase in GHG emissions among the Annex I countries, with 110.4% upsurge during the 1990–2013 period (Turhan et al., 2016). Turkey did not accede to Copenhagen Accord, which was presented at the United Nations Climate Summit in 2009, with a view to reducing GHGs in a nonbinding fashion and which had been based on "targets for developed country" and "voluntary pledges by main developing countries." Unless international climate talks yield binding resolutions, Turkey continues to abstain from pursuing an effective fight against climate change in national and international arenas.

NONALIGNMENT WITH THE EU'S POSITION ON CLIMATE POLICY

The European Union has been characterized as a leader in the international climate struggle. European policy makers introduced goals for the year 2020 in a number of different sectors. In the energy sector, the 2020 goals were based on the three pillars leading European energy policy: security of supply, competitive markets, and sustainability. The 2020 energy goals are to have a 20% reduction in CO_2 emissions compared to 1990 levels, 20% of the energy, on the basis of consumption, coming from renewables and a 20% increase in energy efficiency. Accession negotiations between Turkey and the EU were launched in 2005, and Chapter 27 on Environment and Climate Change has been open since 2009. Climate change and related issues were not on the agenda of Turkish–European relations in the 1990s.

Progress reports of the first years did not even mention climate change or any topic related to harmonization measures. Since 2007, developments on the approximation of environmental legislation regarding climate change issues have begun to diversify. Turkey's harmonization efforts are paired with her positions in international negotiations on climate change. Progress reports between 2002 and 2009 drew attention to the fact that Turkey did not sign the Kyoto Protocol. The Kyoto Protocol is part of the EU's acquis Communautaire; therefore, its adoption is part of the joining process.

Regarding alignment with the EU climate acquis, Turkey is preparing to set up and implement a monitoring, reporting, and verification system and build up its capacity on land use, forestry, and fluorinated gases. Turkey has to develop a comprehensive policy and strategy consistent with the EU 2030 framework. It needs to become consistent with the EU 2030 framework, and it should be well integrated into all relevant sectoral policies. The lack of an overall GHG emissions target, however, constitutes a barrier to the further development of Turkey's carbon market mechanisms. Similarly, the lack of comprehensive and scientific research on the impacts of climate change in Turkey limits the integration of adaptation measures to sector policies and is a reason to underestimate the consequences of changes in climatic conditions.

Regarding commitments under the UN Framework Convention on Climate Change, Turkey submitted its seventh National Communication and its National Inventory in 2018. Pending ratification, Turkey has yet to become one of the Parties, but once it joins, Turkey will face difficulties in complying with the pledge and review process that serves as the legally binding component of the Paris Agreement. In addition to undertaking and communicating INDCs (Intended Nationally Determined Contributions) based on its pledge and review approach, the agreement also sets up a strong and comprehensive transparency framework that builds upon the UNFCCC's existing monitoring, reporting, and reviewing mechanisms, tightening them in such a way as to require greater accountability from Parties (Mazlum, 2017).

Although climate policy diffusion (most notably from the EU) played a certain role in consolidating interest in this period, national developmental aspirations always overwrote climate policy ambitions. The Turkish government established the Climate Change Coordination Committee in 2010, enabling the wider participation of government agencies in the development and implementation of climate change measures. Turkey's National Climate Action Plan for 2011–2023 sets out targets for different sectors such as energy, transportation, industry, waste, agriculture, and forestry. However, it did not foresee national emission reduction goals and all targets are nonbinding.

Şahin (2016) relates Turkey's hesitant climate policies to five factors: (1) economic growth is primarily what fuels the rapid growth in emissions; (2)

energy production has been increasing along with economic growth; (3) the intensity of emissions from energy production has not changed; (4) national energy policy has made coal the preferred fuel for expanding Turkey's energy production capacity; and, (5) therefore, the energy-economy nexus is strongly dependent on fossil fuels, thus creating a constant rise in emissions.

As a matter of global governance, city administrations are taking the lead in tackling climate change with the support of various partners such as WMCCC (World Mayors Council on Climate Change), and C40 (Climate Leadership group) ICLEI and UCLG. In Turkey, however, local governments have been hesitant to take on climate change as a policy priority (Talu, 2015). They are not active players in the energy sector as the system is highly centralized at the national level, despite the privatization processes. Few municipalities are undertaking small-scale renewable energy investments and interact with renewable energy cooperatives. Yet despite being latecomers, the number of municipalities embarking on climate change-related actions has grown steadily over the past five years. For most of these municipalities, stimulation came from contacts with international funding mechanisms and campaigns. As of 2020, fourteen Turkish municipalities with different sizes (from small towns to metropolitan cities) are signatories to the Covenant of Mayors.

CLIMATE-ENERGY NEXUS

Turkish energy policy has never been in line with the country's climate policy. While there were few competing discourses paving the way for a national energy policy such as "energy interdependence," "energy corridor," and "energy terminal," the emphasis of climate policy has been persistently on "special circumstances" of a developing country. Developmentalist approach based on a carbon economy did not take growing concerns of the environment and climate into account. Climate policy requires serious political and institutional support. Regrettably, it cannot enjoy the backing of a renewable energy sector which is quite weak for the moment, whereas fossil fuel energy regulations are very much in line with private interests. States and fossil fuel companies may build strong alliances on legislative issues, subsidies, and weakening the targets of international climate agreements. Turkey is unwilling to comply with international climate agreements and taking only small steps to decarbonize its economy. The IPC (2015) scenario for Turkey to fulfill its responsibility regarding the 2°C target is that its annual CO_2 emissions should reach a peak level of 390 $MtCO_2$ by 2020 and gradually should decrease thereafter down to 340 $MtCO_2$ (the 2010 level) by 2030. The report calls for three main policy instruments in order to meet the 2°C target:

- Carbon tax
- Use of carbon tax revenues for electricity generation from renewables by means of a renewable energy investment fund
- Autonomous efficiency gains (i.e., depending on technological advances and market conditions, and not on any deliberate energy efficiency policies)

As of March 2021, Turkey is yet to formally ratify the Paris agreement alongside Eritrea, Iran, Iraq, Libya, and Yemen. International Energy Agency, in a recent report (2020), assesses the impact of COVID-19 pandemic on clean energy transition and puts forward the idea that the pandemic is having a major impact on energy systems by curbing investments and threatening to slow the expansion of key clean energy technologies. In addition, the current depreciation of Turkish currency and the fact that energy imports account for nearly half of the foreign trade deficit may obstruct the energy transformation needed for climate endeavors. Savaşan (2019) also points out the necessity of the Climate Change Act, which will deal specifically with climate change mitigation and adaptation and draws up the requirements for the national adaptation program, risk assessment, and the reporting/monitoring processes.

REFERENCE

Aksu, C., Erensü, S., and Evren, E. (2016) *Sudan Sebepler: Türkiye'de Neoliberal Su-Enerji Politikaları ve Direnişleri*. İstanbul: İletişim Yayınları.

Aktar C. and Baykan, B.G. (2012) The Administrative and Legal Tools of Developmentt Policy Are Not Environmentally Friendly, BETAM Research Brief 12/138. Bahçeşehir University Center for Economic and Social Research.

Bayraktar, A. (2018) Energy Transition in Turkey. *Turkish Policy Quarterly*, Fall 2018.

Eren, A. (2017) The Political Ecology of Uncertainty: The Production of Truth by Juridical Practices in Hydropower Development. *Journal of Political Ecology* 24, 386–405.

Erensü, S. (2018). Powering Neoliberalization: Energy and Politics in the Making of a New Turkey. *Energy Research & Social Science* 41, 148–157.

Hamsici, M (2011) *Dereler ve İsyanlar*. Nota Bene Yayınları.

HEAL (2014) The Unpaid Health Bill: How Coal Power Plants Make Us Sick. https://www.env-health.org/IMG/pdf/heal_report_the_unpaid_health_bill_how_coal_power_plants_make_us_sick_final.pdf

IEA-Intenational Energy Agency (2020) Country Profile: Turkey. https://www.iea.org/countries/turkey.

IEA-Intenational Energy Agency (2020) The Covid-19 Crisis and Clean Energy Progress. https://www.iea.org/articles/the-impact-of-the-covid-19-crisis-on-clean-energy-progress (Accessed: 07 July 2020).

IPC (2016) Coal Report: Turkey's Coal Policies Related to Climate Change, Economy and Health, https://ipc.sabanciuniv.edu/Content/Images/Document/coal-report-turkeys-coal-policies-related-to-climate-change-economy-and-health-b509f8/coal-report-turkeys-coal-policies-related-to-climate-change-economy-and-health-b509f8.pdf (Accessed: 27 July 2020).

Kaygusuz, K. and Arsel, M. (2005) Energy Politics and Policy. In Adaman, F. and Arsel, M. (Eds.), *Environmentalism in Turkey: Between Democracy and Development*. Ashgate.

Mazlum, S.C. (2017) Turkey and Post-Paris Climate Change Politics: Still Playing Alone. *New Perspectives on Turkey* 56, 145–152.

Ministry of Energy and Natural Resources (2014) National Renewable Energy Action Plan For Turkey https://enerjiapi.etkb.gov.tr//Media/Dizin/EIGM/Mevzuat/253490-national-renewable-energy-action-for-turkey.pdf (Accessed: 15 July 2020).

Pachauri, R.K., and Reisinger, A. (2007) Climate Change 2007: Synthesis Report. Contribution of Working Groups I, II and III to the Fourth Assessment Report of the Intergovernmental Panel on Climate Change. Geneva: IPCC.

Pamir, N (2017) *Enerjinin İktidarı*. İstanbul: Hayy Kitap.

Şahin, Ü. (2016) Warming a Frozen Policy: Challenges to Turkey's Climate Politics after Paris. *Turkish Policy Quarterly* 15(2),117–129.

Savaşan, Z. (2019) Climate Governance in Turkey: A Forward-looking Perspective. *Turkish Studies* 20(4), 541–571.

Talu, N. (2015) *Türkiye'de İklim Değişikliği Siyaseti*. Ankara: Phoenix.

TENVA (2020) Türkiye'nin kurulu gücü 92.097 MW'a ulaştı. http://www.tenva.org/turkiyenin-kurulu-gucu-92-097-mwa-ulasti/ (Accessed: 20 July 2020).

TMMOB (2020) Enerji Görünümü 2020 Oda Raporu, https://www.mmo.org.tr/kitaplar/turkiyenin-enerji-gorunumu-2020 (Accessed: 10 August 2020).

Turhan, E., Cerit-Mazlum, S., Şahin, U., Sorman, A.H., Gundoğan, A.C. (2006) Beyond Special Circumstances: Climate Change Policy in Turkey 1992–2015. *Wiley Interdisciplinary Reviews Climate Change* 7, 448–460.

WWF and IPC (2015) Low Carbon Development Pathways and Priorities for Turkey Climate-Friendly Development in Turkey: A Macro Level Evaluation https://wwftr.awsassets.panda.org/downloads/turkiye_nin_duuk_karbonlu_kalknma_yollar_eng.pdf?5060 (Accessed: 16 July 2020).

Chapter 7

Renewable Energy, Electricity Production, and Economic Growth in the Middle East

Gülfer Vural

ABSTRACT

Energy lies in the focus of economics and politics. Each country is seeking to obtain an appropriate energy policy. Energy is essential for economic growth, but, on the other hand, global warming and climate change are two very important issues that no country can ignore. Since the carbon emissions from fossil fuels cause global warming and climate change, countries tend to employ renewable energy resources due to rapid increase in electricity demand and the environmental concerns. Contribution of renewable energy in promoting economic growth has been assessed in many studies. In this chapter, electricity production with renewable energy resources and economic growth in the Middle East are analyzed. In the history Middle East has been attracted attentions due to its strategic location for energy resources. Middle East countries are Bahrain, Iran, Iraq, Israel, Jordan, Kuwait, Lebanon, Oman, Qatar, Palestine, Saudi Arabia, Turkey, Syria, UAE, and Yemen. The region is an important supplier of the world's oil and gas. The region is also rich in terms of renewable energy resources especially solar and wind.

Keywords: Renewable Energy, Electricity Production, Economic Growth, Middle East

INTRODUCTION

Energy is essential for economic activity and economic growth. There is a strong connection between energy usage and economic growth. Fossil fuels comprise the major source of energy in many countries. Energy usage brings some harmful effects on the environment. Fossil fuels release greenhouse gases and damage the environment by causing climate change and global warming. Many countries suffer from the effects of climate change and global warming by having very high temperatures, lower rainfalls, sea level rises, and their endangering effects on the environment and lives. In order to avoid harmful effects of fossil fuels, countries have started to search alternative clean energy sources after Kyoto Protocol (1997) and Paris Agreement (2015). Renewable energy appears as an environmentally friendly option. The energy-growth nexus has been studied extensively in the literature and studies depict the role of renewable energy in boosting economic growth for many countries. Some of the studies show that renewable energy can be a locomotive for economic growth. Although fossil fuels face the probability of extinction, renewable energy resources can be replenished and never run out. The focus of this chapter is to examine Middle East countries in terms of renewable energy resources and policies and the impact of renewable energy on economic growth for these countries.

The Middle East has a very strategic position in the center of Asia, Europe, and Africa. According to International Energy Agency (IEA), the region includes the Arab countries in the Levant (Lebanon, Syria, Jordan, Israel, and Palestine), the countries on the Arabian Peninsula (Saudi Arabia, Kuwait, Iraq, Bahrain, Qatar, the United Arab Emirates, Oman, and Yemen), Iran and Turkey.

The Middle East is a great supplier of oil and gas that constitute a big portion of their income. The region has challenges in terms of security, sustainability, and energy resources (Khatib, 2014). Saudi Arabia, Kuwait, United Arabian Emirates (UAE), Iran, and Iraq have the largest oil reserves in the world (Ross, 2001), with more than 50% of total oil reserves in the world. In addition, the region is also rich in terms of natural gas reserves. Iran and Qatar are also the two leading natural gas producers of the world.

According to EIA's International Energy Statistics Database, energy consumption has been increased by 20% during 2010–2016. Energy demand in the Middle East is expected to rise at approximately 1.9% annually until 2035 (Camos et al., 2018). Increasing population growth rates, high economic growth rates, and rising living standards make electricity as the region's rapidly growing energy commodity. People need air-conditioning during summers due to an extremely hot climate and this also contributes to the importance of electricity (Zhang et al. 2017).

RENEWABLE ENERGY RESOURCES AND POTENTIAL OF THE MIDDLE EAST

Renewable energy is obtained from solar, wind, biomass, hydro, and geothermal. Solar power is obtained by converting sunlight into electricity and it employs energy from sunlight directly or indirectly. Photovoltaic (PV) technology directly employs the sunlight, and concentrated solar power (CSP) indirectly uses the sunlight through lenses and mirrors. Wind turbines generate wind power that is widely delivered and requires little land. Organic materials from plants and animals, such as wood, food crops, woody plants, agricultural or forest residuals, and organic parts of municipal and industrial wastes form the sources for biomass. Hydropower obtains energy from moving water. Geothermal energy makes use of heat from hot water and steam reservoirs in the earth. Wind, solar, and water-based resources produce no emissions; on the other hand, biomass and geothermal energy generate significantly lower emissions than fossil fuels (El Katiri, 2014, pg7).

Solar energy stands out among the renewable sources in the region. The solar energy in the Middle East and North African countries can supply the world's electricity demand for a long time. Although the solar energy is dominant, the region has great potential in wind, hydro, geothermal power, and biomass. The share of renewable energy in total electricity production is around only 3%, despite the great potential in renewable resources (Bahrampour et al., 2017, pg.2).

Renewable energy investments have been augmenting since 2000s. And in the recent years, several countries have started to make use of renewable energy technologies. Between 2009 and 2012, Israel and UAE are two of the leading countries that invested in renewable energy in the region (Bellakhal et al., 2019, pg.5).

Mostafaeipour and Mostafaeipour (2009) examine electricity production in the Middle East compared with Iran regarding renewable energy. The study reveals that wind and solar energy are more applicable in the region.

The study by Nematollahi et al. (2016) indicates rapidly increasing energy demand and addresses the region's potentials for solar and wind energy. Their findings suggest that the region has great potential for solar and wind energy. Bellakhal et al. (2019) summarize potentials in renewable energy of some countries as follows:

Saudi Arabia: Oil is the main source of energy. Many studies depict the geothermal potential of the country. Wind and solar energy in hybrid systems supply some portion of energy in the evening hours.

UAE: The country has rich resources in terms of oil and gas. Although the country has great potential in solar energy, the dust particles in the air prevent the intensity of solar energy. Low wind speed prevents the usage of wind energy.

Lebanon: Imported fossil fuels are the major source of energy demand. Lebanon is rich in terms of solar energy. In order to decrease the country's energy dependence on imported fossil fuels, renewable energy use should be increased.

Iran: Due to high oil and natural gas reserves, almost 98% of energy demand is met by fossil fuels. Iran has also great wind and solar energy potentials. Hydropower plays a major role in the renewable energy sources, because of the country's geographical location.

Turkey: More than one-third of electricity production is obtained from natural gas that is mostly imported from Russia. Policy makers in Turkey aim to decrease this dependency on imported natural gas. Renewable energy usage is encouraged to reach this aim. Renewable energy sources, mainly hydropower, meet over 30% of the total energy demand. Wind energy investment started in 2006. Although the country has great potential in some regions, share of solar energy is very low in total electricity production.

Table 7.1 presents renewable electricity production as the percentage of total electricity production and CO_2 emissions as metric tons per capita for the years 2000 and 2014 for the Middle East countries. The data are taken from World Bank's World Development Indicators (WDI) database and the year 2014 is the latest one that CO_2 emissions data is available. Palestine is omitted in the table since the CO_2 emission data is missing for 2014. In the region, between 2000 and 2014, the ratio of renewable electricity from renewable sources has not been changed remarkably. Turkey has the highest share of electricity generation from renewable energy. Compared to 2000, in Turkey, Jordan, Lebanon, and Syria the same ratio has decreased while in Iran, Iraq, Israel, and UAE the ratio has increased in the year 2014. The ratio has not been changed for the rest of the countries in the region. The table shows that the region does not utilize its potential in renewable energy. As the table shows, CO_2 emissions are very high for many countries in the region

Table 7.1 Renewable Electricity Production and CO_2 Emissions

	Renewable Electricity Production as % of Total Electricity Production		*CO_2 Emissions (Metric Tons per Capita)*	
Country	*2000*	*2014*	*2000*	*2014*
Saudi Arabia	0.00	0.00	14.37	19.44
Turkey	24.94	20.89	3.42	4.48
Bahrain	0.00	0.00	28.05	23.46
Iran	3.04	5.20	5.67	8.38
Iraq	1.92	4.33	3.08	4.89
Jordan	0.57	0.36	3.03	2.97
Israel	0.07	1.51	9.58	7.86
Kuwait	0.00	0.00	26.19	25.85
Lebanon	4.64	1.08	3.97	3.84
Oman	0.00	0.00	9.65	15.19
Qatar	0.00	0.00	58.62	43.86
Syria	12.81	11.11	3.11	1.64
Yemen	0.00	0.00	0.84	0.88
UAE	0.00	0.26	35.92	22.94

Source: World Development Indicators.

compared to other regions of the world. High amount of CO_2 is released due to power generation.

ADVANTAGES OF RENEWABLE ENERGY

In the long run, the payoff from renewable energy will be more than fossil fuels. Jalilvand (2012) summarizes the benefits of renewable energy as follows: Since in the region electricity consumptions are highly subsidized, employing renewable energy may be seemed useless, but when the environmental costs are taken into consideration, the costs of fossil fuels are tremendous. People suffer both economically and sociologically from the effects of climate change. Climate change results in high temperatures. The record high temperatures cause floods, droughts, extinction of both water resources and arable agricultural areas, and it also damage fishery industry. Because of droughts, people have very severe income loss and even face hunger. The region is generally poor in terms of water resources and this situation forces people to migrate to other regions. Furthermore, renewable energy generation costs have been decreasing with the advancements in technology.

By employing great potential in renewable energy, Middle East countries can also export renewable energy. It will be enough to use only less than 0.2% of area installed with CSP to supply 15% of European electricity demand in 2050 (Trieb et al. 2012). In addition, these countries can employ energy from renewable sources for domestic use and therefore they can export more fossil fuels.

Renewable energy also contributes in terms of energy security issues. Energy security is related to have reliable and affordable energy. Fossil fuel prices depend on many outside factors and fluctuate a lot. Especially countries that have no fossil fuel resources can make use of economic and stable energy by employing renewable energy.

Another advantage of renewable energy generation is creating new jobs in these countries. Zwaan (2013) evaluated the creation of renewable energy jobs in the region and estimated a potential of 155,000 direct and 115,000 indirect jobs.

In the rural areas of less developed countries, electricity does not reach people. Renewable energy can contribute to the electrification of remote rural areas, too.

RENEWABLE ENERGY POLICIES IN THE MIDDLE EAST

Because of the government policies, the region does not utilize sufficient renewable energy despite the great potential and advantages of the renewable energy. Therefore in the region, policy makers should play active roles and subsidize renewable energy investments.

El Katiri (2014) argues that the energy pricing mechanism in the region prevents a reasonable cost comparison between the renewable energy and the fossil fuels. The main reason behind not employing sufficient renewable sources lies in the specific electricity market structure of the region (El Katiri, 2014, pg.10–11). The study summarizes impediments for renewable energy deployment in Middle East and North African countries. First, since electricity prices are highly subsidized, very low electricity prices for households and industries are charged in the region. Second, the renewable energy costs become uncompetitive against underpricing and subsidies of domestic fossil fuels. The study points out that after a reform in domestic energy pricing, renewable energy will be used more in the region.

RENEWABLE ENERGY AND ECONOMIC GROWTH

Energy is an input in the production and provides employment opportunities to many people. Renewable energy is an alternative to fossil fuels for economic growth while decreasing greenhouse gas emissions and keeping the environment clean. Advancing technology makes renewable energy more affordable by decreasing costs. After the Paris Conference (2015), 164 countries exist with renewable energy targets. IRENA (2016) report points out the importance of renewable energy on economic growth globally. IRENA's analysis shows that renewable energy contributes to economic growth in oil importer countries positively. On the other hand, since fossil fuel export accounts an important portion of the national income in oil exporter countries, renewable energy results in decrease in GDP. The analysis estimates the effects of doubling the share of renewables in total energy mix by 2030 on global GDP as between 0.6% and 1.1%. It is estimated for Japan at 2.3%. For Australia, Brazil, Germany, South Korea, Mexico, and South Africa more than 1% positive impacts are estimated. For China, France, India, the United Kingdom, and the United States, the impact is estimated positive but less than 1%. For oil-exporting countries, such as Saudi Arabia, Russia, Nigeria, and Venezuela, a decrease in GDP is estimated. By 2030, improvements in renewable energy technologies can provide lower electricity prices. The decline in electricity prices results in decrease in inflation, increase in real incomes, and promote economic activity. Investment goods and service sectors (construction, manufacturing, engineering sectors) will benefit more from increase in renewable energy (IRENA, 2016).

Institutions are essential for economic growth. Saidi et al. (2019) argue that, although the Middle East and North Africa regions are rich in renewable energy resources, institutional quality is a big concern in these regions. They explore renewable energy economic growth nexus by taking institutional quality into account during 1986–2015. Corruption, bureaucracy quality, democracy accountability, law and order, and ethnic tensions are used as institutional variables. Their empirical results indicate that improvements in institutional quality will stimulate renewable energy investments and economic growth.

Bellakhal et al. (2009) investigate the link between trade openness, governance, and renewable energy investment in the Middle East and North Africa. They note that for the renewable energy investment, two risks, namely regulatory risk and political risk, are identified. The empirical findings indicate that high institutional quality is related with renewable energy investment for MENA countries.

CONCLUSION

In this chapter, renewable energy production and the link between renewable energy and economic growth are assessed for the Middle East countries. Fast-growing population and economic growth increase electricity demand. According to the studies, the region has great potential renewable energy especially in solar and wind energy. The solar energy in the region is sufficient to meet the world's total electricity demand for several years. Despite the extreme potential in renewable energy, the region does not utilize it efficiently. The underlying reason is the governments' policies. Highly subsidized electricity prices by the governments arise as the main impediments for the usage of renewable resources. Taking economic and environmental benefits of renewable energy into account, in the long run, usage of renewable energy will be more useful. Due to current fossil fuel-based power generation, high CO_2 emissions occur in many countries in the region. Renewable energy resources release no carbon emissions or very little emissions. Renewable energy can promote economic growth, create new employment opportunities, and provide electricity to remote rural areas by keeping the environment clean. Policy makers should develop renewable energy strategies and subsidize investments in renewable energy.

REFERENCES

Bahrampour, Hamid, Beheshti, Amirkhosro, Askari, Mohammad Bagher and Bahrampour, Mohammad (2017). "Evaluation of Renewable Energies Production Potential in the Middle East: Confronting the World's Energy Crisis." *Frontiers in Energy* 1–15. 10.1007/s11708-017-0486-2.

Bellakhal, Rihab, Ben Kheder, Sonia and Haffoudhi, Houda (2019). "Governance and renewable energy investment in MENA countries: How does trade matter?" *Energy Economics*, 84, 104541.

Camos, Daniel, Bacon, Robert, Estache, Antonio and Hamid, Mohamad M. (2018). *Shedding Light on Electricity Utilities in the Middle East and North Africa: Insights from a Performance Diagnostic. Directions in Development—Energy and Mining*. Washington, DC: World Bank.

El Katiri, Laura (2014). *A Roadmap for Renewable Energy in the Middle East and North Africa*. Oxford Institute for Energy Studies.

IRENA (2016). *International Renewable Energy Agency, "Renewable Energy Benefits: Measuring The Economics*. Abu Dhabi: IRENA.

Jalilvand, David Ramin (2012). *Renewable Energy for the Middle East and North Africa: Policies for a Successful Transition*. Berlin: Friedrich Ebert Stiftung.

Khatib, H. (2014). "Oil and Natural Gas Prospects: Middle East and North Africa." *Energy Policy* 64, 71–77.

Mostafaeipour, A. and Mostafaeipour, N. (2009). "Renewable Energy Issues and Electricity Production in Middle East Compared with Iran." *Renewable and Sustainable Energy Reviews*, 13, 1641–1645.

Nematollahi, Omid, Hoghooghi, Hadi, Rasti, Mehdi and Sedaghat, Ahmad (2015). "Energy Demands and Renewable Energy Resources in the Middle East." *Renewable and Sustainable Energy Reviews* 54, 1172–1181. 10.1016/j.rser.2015.10.058.

Trieb, F., Schillings, C., Pregger, T., and O'Sullivan, M., (2012). "Solar Electricity Imports from the Middle East and North Africa to Europe." *Energy Policy*. 42, 341–353.

Ross, M.L. (2001) "Does Oil Hinder Democracy?" *World Politics* 53(3), 325–361.

Saidi, H., El Montasser, G. and Ajmi, A.N. (2020). "The Role of Institutions in the Renewable Energy-Growth Nexus in the MENA Region: A Panel Cointegration Approach." *Environmental Modelling and Assessment* 25, 259–276. https://doi.org/10.1007/s10666-019-09672-y.

Shawon, M.J., El Chaar, L. and Lamont, L.A. (2013). "Overview of Wind Energy and Its Cost in the Middle East." *Sustainable Energy Technologies and Assessments*, 2, 1–11. https://doi.org/10.1016/j.seta.2013.01.002.

WDI, World Development Indicators.

Zhang, Xiaoping, Mingyu Ou, Yanmin Song and Xiaolu Li. (2017). "Review of Middle East Energy Interconnection Development." *Journal of Modern Power Systems and Clean Energy* 5, 917–935.

Zwaan, Bob, Cameron, Lachlan and Kober, Tom (2013). "Potential for Renewable Energy Jobs in the Middle East." *Energy Policy* 60, 10.1016/j.enpol.2013.05.014. https://www.eia.gov/international/data/world.

Chapter 8

Analysis of the Renewable Energy Sources for the Middle East Countries

Hatice Kerra Geldi

ABSTRACT

This study aims to analyze the renewable energy sources of the Middle East region, which is one of the major actors of the global energy market. Clean energy sources such as renewable energy have started to gain greater importance, as the recent developments on the world's agenda obligate countries to change their present production and consumption patterns. Besides its abundant fossil fuel supply, the region has significant potential for renewable energy sources, especially for solar and wind energies. Current trends show that the region is far away from its potential. Hence, there is an ample opportunity for renewable energy generation in the region if countries can successfully align their social, political, and economic dynamics.

Keywords: Renewable Sources; Electricity; Middle East

INTRODUCTION

What the earth signals us through global warming, climate crisis, and several kinds of pandemics is that the past and present production and consumption patterns of humankind are not compatible with the environment and also not sustainable. The present global warming and climate crisis also necessitate the consideration of the world's energy landscape not only in the domain of natural sciences but also in terms of social, economic, and political systems (Penna, 2020). Together with the organized global efforts to fight climate change, significant volatility on oil and gas prices, the emergence of new sources of oil and gas such as shale gas and coal bed methane, and the evolution of renewable energy technologies make up the main headlines of the scope of the world's energy.

The current global energy use mainly depends on the nonrenewable energy sources of fossil fuels such as coal, oil and natural gas, and uranium[1] that constitute nuclear power. However, there exist two drawbacks related to non-renewable energy sources. First, these sources have a finite supply. Hence, continuous depletion of these energy sources will eventually result in an energy shortage for the world. The second and the most alarming drawback is that these mineral energy sources result in the emission of an increasing number of toxic elements such as methane, nitrous oxide, and carbon dioxide (CO_2) that are the primary greenhouse gases (GHGs) responsible for climate change. Both the drawbacks urge us to search for alternative energy sources that will decrease GHG emissions, mitigate global warming, and solve the energy supply problem.

One of the proposed alternative clean energy sources is nuclear energy. There are 440 nuclear reactors in thirty countries at present, although the recent catastrophe at Fukushima (Japan) in 2011 has raised concerns about the safety of this energy source. While the United States is the leading country with ninety-five reactors, it is followed by France and China that has fifty-seven and forty-seven reactors, respectively (statista, 2020). Although nuclear energy is proposed as one of the clean energy sources with its low carbon emissions, it involves potential negative externality on the environment due to the radioactive and hazardous waste generation.

Another proposed solution for the world's energy problem is to decrease the current dominance of mineral sources on energy production and shift toward renewable sources such as biomass, hydropower, wind, and solar energy. Between 1990 and 2018, while the world's energy supply has grown by 1.8%, renewable energy resources have grown 2% yearly. In 2018, renewable energy sources made up 13.5% of the world's total energy supply. Among the renewable resources, the annual growth rate of solar photovoltaic (PV) is the highest at 36.5%, which is followed by the growth of wind power by 23%. In 2018, while coal accounted for 38.2% of global electricity generation, renewable energy sources accounted for 25.2%, which is slightly higher than the contribution of natural gas (23.1%) (IEA, 2020).

Technological developments in renewable energy generation support this trend. These developments have resulted in a continuing decline in costs for each renewable source. The global weighted-average cost of electricity declined by 26% for concentrated solar power (CSP), 14% for bioenergy, 13% for solar PV and onshore wind, 12% for hydropower, and 1% for geothermal and offshore wind in 2018 (IRENA, 2019). Hence, these cost declines make renewable power more competitive and lower-cost option against fossil fuels. In this respect, the usual argument against renewable sources in developing countries as a "luxury" source for energy generation holds less and less accurate (Bellakhal et al., 2019).

The present study focuses on the Middle East (ME) region,[2] as the region has a significant role in the global energy framework. Despite the potential for renewable energy sources, the region still relies mainly on nonrenewable energy sources. The ME is the world's largest oil producer. In 2019, the region's proved oil reserves were estimated as 833.8 billion barrels, making up 48.1% of the global total, and the region's proved natural gas reserves are estimated as 75.6 trillion cubic meters, making up 38.0% of the global total (BP, 2020). Both figures show that the region is the primary supplier of the oil and natural gas markets. In the region, while Iran, Iraq, Saudi Arabia, Syria, and United Arab Emirates[3] are traditional energy exporters, Egypt, Israel, Jordan, Lebanon, and Turkey are traditional energy importers. While Saudi Arabia has the largest proved oil reserves (17.2% of the global total), followed by Iran (9% of the global total) and Iraq (8.4% of the global total), Iran has the largest proved natural gas reserves (16.1% of the global total). However, as the majority of electricity production and heat generation is from natural gas, natural gas consumption is growing faster than oil consumption in the region. Therefore, the ME is likely to lose its exporter role and become a large net importer of natural gas before 2060 (Farzaneh et al., 2016).

Together with the depletion of fossil fuels, another energy-related issue for the ME is the substantial volatility in oil and gas prices. The significant revenue loss due to a fall in oil prices[4] since mid-2014 has harmed the fiscal balances of oil-exporting countries of the region, requiring them to reform their energy policies. On the other hand, energy-importing countries cannot fully benefit from low energy prices due to internal and external issues related to ongoing wars and political turmoil in the region.[5] Furthermore, the increasing population of these countries,[6] higher standards of living, and growth in energy-intensive industries bring the problem of the fulfillment of growing energy demand for the ME. Hence to be able to analyze the energy systems of these countries, we have to take into account social, political, and economic circumstances. Depending on these country-specific factors, the importance of energy security, economic development, energy access, and concern for climate and health will vary for each country (Griffiths, 2017).

Given this background on the multidimensional energy-related concerns for the region, the present study aims to analyze the renewable energy sources of the ME region as several studies highlight the positive effects of clean energy systems such as renewable energy. This effects can be classified as decreasing GHG emissions, coping with the climate change, reducing fossil fuel dependence, addressing energy security issues, meeting excessive energy demand, and promoting the growth and sustainable development (Apergis & Payne, 2011; Trieb et al., 2012; Al-Mulali et al., 2013; Farhani, 2013; Pao et al., 2014; Kahia et al., 2019). For example, Kahia et al. (2017) indicate bidirectional causality between renewable energy and economic growth for net oil-importing countries of the ME and North Africa region. Moreover, El Fadel et al. (2013) find a significant decrease in both GHG emissions and the cost of electricity generation with the increase in the share of renewable energy in the ME. By applying zero emissions scenario, Farzaneh et al. (2016), on the other hand, estimate renewable and nuclear energies can supply nearly 43% of the global energy of the ME region by 2100.

TRENDS IN RENEWABLE ENERGY FOR THE ME

In the ME region, renewable energy started to develop mainly in the early 2000s. The region has a significant potential for renewable energy resources,[7] especially solar and wind resources, but currently, these renewable sources contribute only 4% to the region's primary energy consumption (BP, 2020). Figure 8.1 shows the electricity generation trend for renewable energy during the period 2000–2018. Until the late 2000s, the main component of renewable energy was the hydropower (led mainly by Turkey, Egypt, and Iran). The last decade has experienced the gradual introduction of other renewable resources, with the increasing importance of solar PV, onshore wind, and geothermal energy. In the given period, Turkey increased electricity generated from renewable sources to approximately 97.8 TWh in 2018 from 31.2 TWh in 2000. Thus, the share of renewable energy in Turkey's electricity generation increased from 25 to 32%.

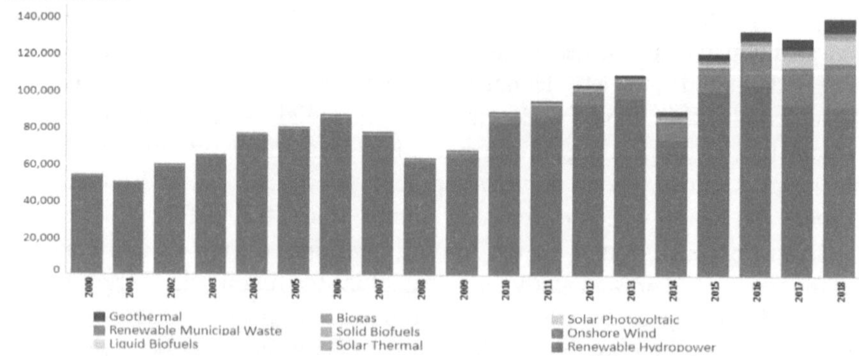

Figure 8.1 Trends in renewable energy (electricity generation) for the selected ME countries. *Source*: (IRENA statistics).

All other countries of the region do have smaller shares of renewable energy electricity generation when compared with Turkey, so it shows that they are not using much of their potential for renewable energy sources. For the region, the second country that takes advantage of renewable resources on electricity generation is Jordan, as it increased its share from 0.6 to 10.9% (i.e., with an approximately 18-fold increase) in the given period. For the rest of the countries, the share of electricity generation by renewable sources for the years 2000 and 2018 (in the same order) are as follows: Egypt (20.1% and 8.1%), Iran (3.1% and 5.4%), Iraq (1.9% and 2.1%), Israel (0.1% and 2.5%), Lebanon (9.2% and 3.8%), and Syria (12.9% and 3.6%). UAE started to employ renewable energy sources relatively late when it is compared with other countries. While electricity produced from renewable sources was 0.01% in 2009, this share increased to approximately 1% in 2018. As the largest oil producer, Saudi Arabia has insignificant shares of renewable energy generation, reaching to the maximum share of 0.06% in 2018.

The same trend also holds for the installed capacity (see Figure 8.2). The period shows that there is a significant increase in solar PV capacity, which is followed by a capacity increase in onshore wind energy, especially since 2010. The driving country for the region's increasing trend in renewable energy is again Turkey. Nearly 49% of electricity installed capacity came from renewable energy sources in 2019. Jordan again follows Turkey, as the share of its renewable energy was 25.8% last year.

While Syria and Iran each has a share of 15%, approximately 9% of Egypt's and Lebanon's total electricity installed capacity derives from renewable energy sources in 2019. These countries are followed by Israel (8%), Iraq (7%), and UAE (6%). Saudi Arabia has a minor share in the

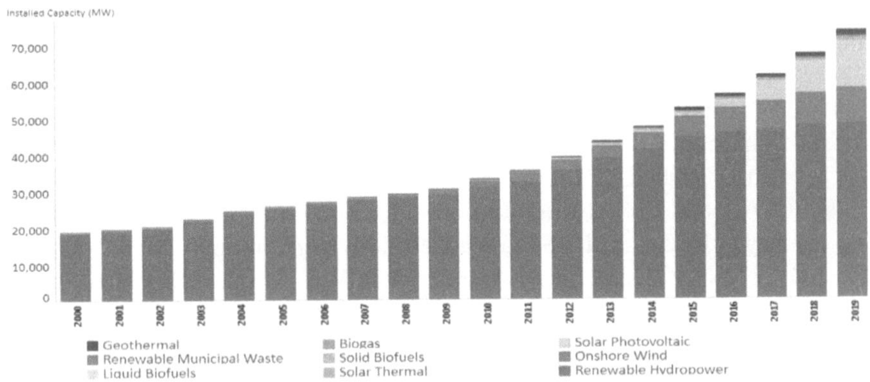

Figure 8.2 Trends in renewable energy (installed capacity) for the selected ME countries. *Source*: (IRENA statistics).

renewable energy contribution to installed capacity again, as it was 0.5% in 2019.

SOLAR ENERGY

The sun, as the world's infinite and prime source of energy, is awaiting to be used. The annual amount of solar radiation that the earth receives is approximately 900 million terawatt-hours, and it is more than 7,500 times the world's total annual primary energy consumption. As Penna (2020, p.192) states, "The technological revolution of the half century would have stalled without increasingly powerful arrays of solar panels [used in space applications]." While China is the leading solar PV supplier, it dominates the solar energy market together with Japan, India, the United Kingdom, and the United States. Although the ME region does not have a significant share in the global solar energy market, it has excellent potential for all forms of solar energy generation.

For the ME region, two drivers of the accelerating solar energy applications are solar PV and CSP, in order of their significance. This pattern is in line with the solar energy endowment of the region and a decrease in technology costs. In the region, Direct Normal Irradiance (DNI),[8] as a measure of the suitability for solar power applications such as CSP[9] and solar heating and cooling, has an average value of 2,200 kWh/m^2/year. Region's Global Horizontal Irradiance (GHI) as a measure of the suitability for solar PV technologies is also very good ranging between 1,920 kWh/m^2/year in Lebanon to 2,450 kWh/m^2/year in Egypt (Griffiths, 2017). Hence, the region is one of the best places for solar energy generation.

Figure 8.3 studies the electricity generation by solar energy (including on-grid solar PV, off-grid solar PV, and CSP) between the years 2010 and 2018, as the accumulation of solar energy accelerates after 2010. Turkey is the leading country on the solar energy electricity generation for the given period. While Turkey generated 8.5 GWh electricity in 2010, this value increased to 7,803 GWh (or 7.803 TWh) in 2018. Turkish solar energy generation mainly depends on solar PV as the share of CSP in total solar energy is 0.04% in 2018. For the solar PV, Turkey is followed by Israel (1,573 GWh), Jordan (1,475 GWh), and United Arab Emirates (1,076 GWh). For the CSP, the leading country is Egypt, with 484 GWh electricity generation in 2018, followed by UAE (233 GWh), and Saudi Arabia (149 GWh). On the other hand, Israel (11 GWh) and Turkey (3 GWh) have minor shares for the CSP contribution of renewable energy electricity generation.

For the ME group, Israel led the market in new additions to CSP plants as the global CSP capacity increased by 11% in 2019 (REN21, 2020). Two new projects of CSP (Megalim and Negev) are the first two commercial

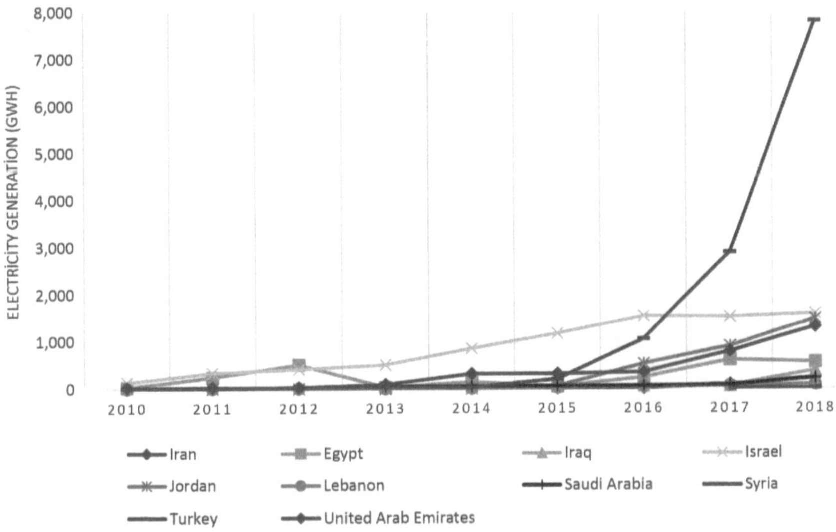

Figure 8.3 Accumulation of the amount of solar energy generation. *Source*: (IRENA statistics).

CSPs and the largest renewable energy plants in Israel. On the other hand, there is commercial CSP capacity under construction in Saudi Arabia and UAE by 2019.

WIND ENERGY

On a global scale, wind turbines provide the increasing shares of energy generation, especially in China, Denmark, Germany, India, and the United States. Wind power is the second growing renewable energy source force in the ME region since 2008. The wind potential of the region mainly derives from Egypt, Iran, Jordan, and Turkey. Figure 8.4 studies the electricity generation of wind energy in the ME during 2006–2018. As in the case of solar energy, Turkey is the leading country in generating electricity from wind power. While Turkey generated 126 GWh of electricity from wind energy in 2006, this value tremendously increased to 19,949 GWh (~20 TWh) in 2018. Distant followers of Turkey are Egypt (2.33 TWh), Jordan (0.72 TWh), and Iran (0.58 TWh) in 2018.

The global wind power market enlarged by 19% in 2019, with around 60 GW of new capacity added to the world's electric grids (REN21, 2020). By 2019, in terms of the installed capacity, the leading country is Turkey (7,591 MW), followed by Egypt (1,375 MW), Jordan (374 MW), and Iran (302 MW). While wind energy made up 7.4% of Turkey's electricity

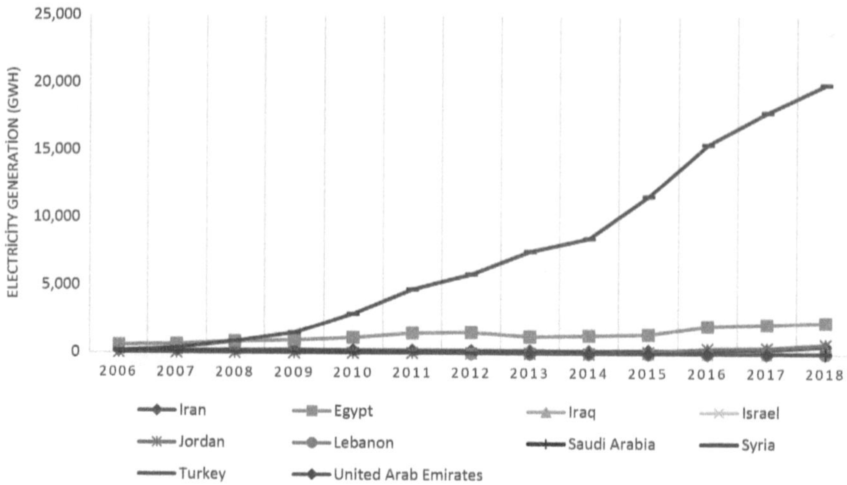

Figure 8.4 Accumulation of the amount of wind energy generation. *Source*: (IRENA statistics).

generation in 2018, wind turbine installations increased to a total of more than 8.1 GW. Egypt's new installation (262 MW) came from the country's largest and first privately owned wind farm. While Jordan and Iran added 200 MW and 50 MW, respectively, in 2019, Saudi Arabia contracted its first large-scale wind farm (Dumat Al Jandal project) to install 400 MW.

HYDROPOWER

While the use of kinetic energy of water saved the workforce of humans and animals in ancient times, the modernization enabled the construction of large dams with powerful turbines that store the water of broad rivers and generate electrical energy (Penna, 2020). In the world, the largest producers of hydropower are Brazil, China, Canada, and the United States. The ME region also has hydropower potential, even though it is not as significant as the solar and wind potential of the region. Figure 8.5 indicates the contribution of hydropower to electricity production between 2000 and 2018. As an early investor, Turkey has been benefiting mainly from the energy-generating power of water. While hydropower made up 99% of total renewable electricity generation in 2000, this share fell to 61% in 2018 as the shares of solar energy and wind energy are increasing. Of the total electricity generated in 2018, 19% is supplied by the hydropower generation in Turkey. Iran and Egypt are following Turkey with 15.76 TWh and 12.73 TWh electricity generation in 2018, respectively.

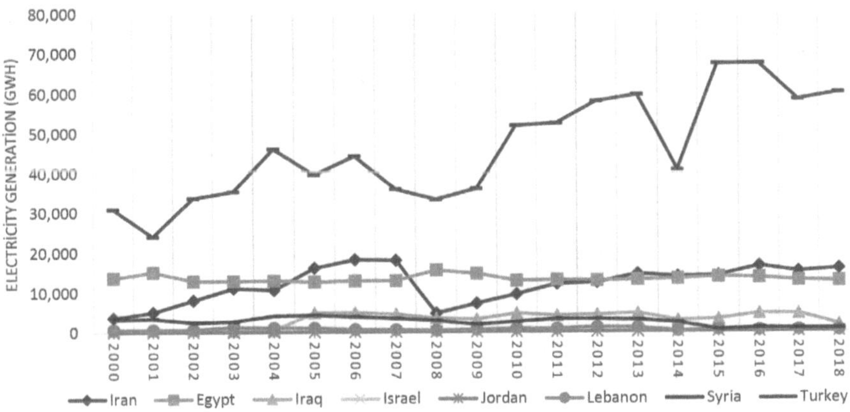

Figure 8.5 Accumulation of the amount of hydropower generation. *Source*: (IRENA statistics).

In the global hydropower market, annual capacity installations continued to decrease in 2018. Besides, the changes in capacity, weather conditions, and local operating conditions result in yearly variations on hydropower generation. In 2019, the estimated annual increase in global hydropower generation was 2.3%, hence making up 15.9% of the world's total electricity generation (REN21, 2020). Turkey is among the top ten countries[10] for total hydropower capacity, all of which represent 66% of global capacity. In 2019, together with suitable hydrological conditions, hydropower generation in Turkey increased to approximately 90 TWh and provided nearly 30% of total electricity supply. In 2019, installed capacities for hydropower for the region are as follows: Egypt (2.8 GW), Iran (12.2 GW), Iraq (2.3 GW), Israel (6.6 MW), Jordan (16.2 MW), Lebanon (253 MW), Syria (1.5 GW), Turkey (28.5 GW) and no hydropower installed capacity for Saudi Arabia and UAE (IRENA, Renewable Energy Statistics 2020).

GEOTHERMAL ENERGY

Except for the case of Turkey, geothermal energy does not constitute a significant part of renewable energy production in the ME region. In 2019, 0.7 GW of new geothermal power generating capacity was estimated, for which Turkey is one of the leading countries, together with Indonesia and Kenya (REN21, 2020). Together with China, Iceland, and Japan, Turkey is also one of the leading countries, accounting for approximately 75% of all geothermal direct use in 2019. In 2018, 7.6% of the total renewable electricity generation and 2.4% of total electricity generation were produced by geothermal energy. Within the group, the countries that have the potential are Israel with 23 MW of geothermal capacity and Saudi Arabia that has geothermal sites with temperatures exceeding 200°C (IRENA & League of Arab States, 2014).

PUBLIC POLICY AND INVESTMENTS

Governmental support for renewable energy market may take several forms: tax credits; the renewables portfolio standard in which suppliers must sell a certain amount of electricity produced by renewable energy source (i.e., providing quantity control); feed-in tariffs in which suppliers sell the electricity of renewable source at a predetermined rate during a given period (i.e., providing price control); and investment subsidies. As it is valid for foreign direct investment, investments in renewable energy are significantly affected by the legal environment, government support schemes, and the ease of doing business. For the selected countries except for Turkey, substantial incentives for renewable energy sources are missing.

In the case of Turkey, the law on the utilization of renewable energy sources (2005) can be seen as the beginning of the incentives of renewable investments (Acar et al., 2019). It included incentives such as exemption from licensing fees, facilitation of land appropriation, and fixed feed-in tariff for a purchase guarantee until 2011. By 2010, a new law was enforced for the utilization of renewable energy sources. It determined different feed-in tariffs for each renewable source. Besides feed-in tariffs in the context of renewable energy support mechanisms, Turkey also performed renewable energy source area auctions in order to allocate public land to install power stations.

Although these countries have high solar energy capacity, there is not a considerable public investment in solar energy. Public investments are made mainly after 2013 (IRENA, IRENA RE Time Series). When total public investments in solar energy are compared from 2010 to 2018, Egypt is the leader with a total investment value of 1.564 billion USD (at 2017 prices). The following countries are Turkey (USD 1.019 billion), Jordan (USD 0.702 billion), Israel (USD 0.597 billion), and Iraq (USD 0.257 billion).

As in the case of solar energy, public investments in wind energy are relatively low for the ME region. Within the group, only Egypt, Jordan, and Turkey have a considerable public investment in wind energy when it is compared with the remaining countries. Egypt's total public investment increased to 1.336 (USD 2017 billion), of which the highest investment (nearly USD 683 million at 2017 prices) was made in the year 2010. While Jordan invested a total amount of 224.8 (USD 2017 billion), Turkey's public investment approached to a total value of 118 (USD 2017 billion) between the years 2000 and 2018.

LEGAL FRAMEWORK THAT GUIDES TOWARD RENEWABLE ENERGY SOURCES

The Paris Agreement (December 12, 2015, Paris) of the United Nations Framework Convention on Climate Change (UNFCCC) mechanism aims to strengthen the global response to fight for climate change and limit carbon emissions to 1.5°C in this century. As of June 2020, 189 countries had ratified the agreement. Among the selected group of ME countries, three of these countries, namely Iran, Iraq, and Turkey, have signed the Paris Agreement, but they have not ratified the agreement.

The ME region, overall, does not have a well-known reputation for carbon emissions. The region is responsible for approximately 7.3% of the global CO_2 emissions in 2019 but has the fastest growth rate in CO_2 emissions (BP, 2020). The average value of the region's per capita carbon emissions is higher than the whole world's CO_2 metric tons per capita value. Although the values are not as high as the world's two largest polluters, namely, China (9,825.8 million tons) and the United States (4,964.7 million tons), Iran has the most substantial volume with 670.7 million tons of emission in 2019. The next two carbon emitter countries are Saudi Arabia and Turkey that released 579.9 and 383.3 million tons of CO_2 in 2019, respectively. UAE (282.6 million tons) and Egypt (217.4 million tons) are following the suit.

To be able to limit carbon emissions, under the Paris Agreement, the ME countries (as all other signatories) have committed to promoting renewable energy and energy efficiency through Intended Nationally Determined Contributions (INDCs) that summarize their intended climate action. While Egypt, Saudi Arabia, and the United Arab Emirates have not made any unconditional GHG emissions reduction commitment[11] in their INDCs, Iran, Iraq, Israel, Jordan, Lebanon, and Turkey have made unconditional commitments (Griffiths, 2017). Table 8.1 shows the conditional and unconditional commitments for these countries. Among the group, Israel is the most motivated country with an unconditional commitment to a 26% reduction in GHG emissions by 2030.

In order to realize their conditional and unconditional commitments on the percentage reduction in GHG emissions, these countries also announce target

Table 8.1 Committed % reduction in GHG emissions by 2030

Country	*Unconditional commitment*	*Conditional commitment*
Iran	4	12
Iraq	13	15
Israel	26	–
Jordan	1.5	14
Lebanon	15	30
Turkey	21	–

Source: Based on UNFCCC, INDCs as communicated by Parties, https://www4.unfccc.int/sites/submissions/INDC/Submission%20Pages/submissions.aspx.

values for the share of renewable sources on electricity generation. While Egypt targets to increase its renewable share to 37–42% by 2035 (REN21, 2020), Iraq and Israel aim to realize 30% as the renewable share by 2030. For the year 2030, the target values of the selected countries are as follows: Israel (17%); Jordan, Lebanon, and Saudi Arabia (each 30%); and Syria (4.3%). On the other hand, UAE aims to increase its share to 44% by 2050. As the forerunner of the selected group of countries on the inclusion of renewable energy sources into its energy composition, Turkey's objective is to raise the percentage of renewable share of electricity generation to 65% by 2023. In the same vein, countries also set their renewable energy targets in terms of the specific amount of installed capacity or electricity generation. Table 8.2 shows these target values for the selected countries.

Table 8.2 Renewable energy target values for installed capacity or generation (as of 2019)

Country	*Technology*	*Target*
Egypt	Hydropower	2.8 GW by 2020
	Solar PV	17.3 GW by 2035
	CSP	1.1 GW by 2020; 11 GW by 2035
	Wind power	7.2 GW by 2022; 21 GW by 2035
Iran	Solar and wind power	5 GW by 2020
Iraq	Solar PV	2.24 GW by 2020
Jordan	Electricity	1.8 GW by 2020; 3.2 GW by 2025
	Bio-power	50 MW by 2025
	Solar PV	1 GW by 2020; 2.5 GW by 2025
	Wind power	1.2 GW by 2020
Lebanon	Wind power	400-500 MW by 2020
Saudi Arabia	Electricity	27.3 GW by 2023; 58.7 GW by 2030
	Geothermal, bio-power (waste-to-energy)	13 GW combined by 2040
	Solar PV	20 GW by 2023; 40 GW by 2030
	CSP	300 MW by 2023; 2.7 MW by 2030
	Wind power	7 GW by 2023; 16 GW by 2030
Syria	Bio-power	140 MW by 2020; 260 MW by 2025; 400 MW by 2030
	Solar PV	380 MW by 2020; 1.1 GW by 2025; 1.8 GW by 2030
	CSP	50 MW by 2025; 1.3 GW by 2030
	Wind power	1 GW by 2020; 1.5 GW by 2025; 2 GW by 2030
Turkey	Bio-power from solid biomass	1 GW by 2023
	Geothermal power	1 GW by 2023
	Hydropower	34 GW by 2023
	Solar PV	5 GW by 2023
	Wind power	20 GW by 2023

Source: (REN21, 2020).

CONCLUSION

Increased awareness and interest for renewable energy sources have mainly initiated with the accelerated concerns about the climate crisis. These concerns have required urgent action plans for all countries, be it developed or developing, in terms of energy production, energy consumption, and sustainability. As one of the leading actors of the global energy market, the ME also has a significant potential for renewable energy sources, especially for solar and wind energies. However, current trends show that the region is far away from its potential. Hence, there is an ample—waiting to be invested—opportunity for renewable energy generation in the region if countries can successfully align their social, political, and economic dynamics.

Besides the possible positive effects of renewable energy sources on climate change, energy security, and sustainable development, renewable energy sources have great importance on several grounds in the ME context. First, the energy policy of the region that puts greater emphasis on renewable energy sources is also tied to the water policy, as the region's scarcity of water and climate conditions result in dependence on energy-intensive methods such as air-conditioning and seawater desalination. In this respect, unified energy and water policy planning is a necessity for the region. Second, another problem for the region is the rise in urbanization. Urbanization is further increasing the energy demand in these countries. Hence, renewable energy potential can be used to meet this excess demand. Finally, in some countries, decentralized electricity generation by renewable sources may solve the problem of low rural electrification rate that results from long distances and severe geographical conditions.

As a final word, although technological developments have facilitated the rapid development of renewable energy markets and decreased the cost of investing in renewable energy sources, regional and international cooperation may ease the transition to more renewable energy-based systems in the ME. This cooperation is possible given the examples of Desertec[12] and Medgrid projects that aim to establish a solar energy link between the EU and North Africa.

NOTES

1. Recent developments on the nuclear energy enable the use of plutonium together with uranium. Future reactors will use plutonium and the following generation will use thorium. Penna (2020) states these developments may solve the depletion problem but warns that mining and manufacturing of cements and industrial-grade steel necessary to build a nuclear power plants still emit huge amounts of CO_2.

2. The ME region in this study covers ten countries: Egypt, Iran, Iraq, Israel, Jordan, Lebanon, Saudi Arabia, Syria, Turkey, and United Arab Emirates (UAE).

3. Iran, Iraq, Saudi Arabia, and United Arab Emirates are members of the Organization of Petroleum Exporting Countries (OPEC).

4. Main factors that push oil prices down are the weaker global growth, the weakening of demand growth from Asia, the availability of new resources (such as strong shale gas production in the United States), temporary waivers for some Iranian oil export sanctions, and the appreciation of the US dollar (Kitous et al., 2016; IMF, 2019).

5. While the Syria is still struggling with the civil war, countries such as Jordan, Lebanon, and Turkey are trying to cope with the refugee crisis from the Syrian war.

6. For the whole group, population growth rate between 2000 and 2019 is 42% (WDI).

7. The region also possesses abundant nonfuel minerals such as barite (in Iran and Turkey), boron (in Turkey), bromine (in Israel and Jordan), clay (in Turkey), gypsum (in Egypt and Iran), iron (in Turkey), iron ore (in Iran), lead (in Egypt and Saudi Arabia), magnesium (in Turkey), marble (in Jordan), phosphate (in Egypt, Iran, Jordan, and Syria), potash (in Israel and Jordan), strontium (in Iran and Turkey), sulfur (in Iran, Saudi Arabia, and UAE), and zinc (in Egypt and Saudi Arabia).

8. DNI is the amount of solar radiation received per unit area by a surface that is perpendicular to the sun rays.

9. As DNI requires perpendicular (or normal) radiation, it makes the location of CSP plants as an important determinant of energy generation.

10. These countries are China, Brazil, Canada, the United States, the Russian Federation, India, Norway, Japan, and France (REN21, 2020).

11. Given the fact that to meet the Paris Agreement climate targets, a third of oil reserves, half of gas reserves, and more than 80% of global coal reserves should remain unused (McGlade & Ekins, 2015), the reluctance of these oil-exporting countries is not unanticipated.

12. Currently, Desertec Industrial Initiative (DII) project failed mainly because of the political instability over North Africa.

REFERENCES

Acar, B., Selcuk, O., & Dastan, S. (2019). The merit order effect of wind and river type hydroelectricity generation on Turkish electricity prices. *Energy Policy*, 132, 1298–1319.

Al-mulali, U., Fereidouni, H., Lee, J., & Sab, C. (2013). Examining the bi-directional long run relationship between renewable energy consumption and GDP growth. *Renewable and Sustainable Energy Reviews*, 22, 209–222.

Apergis, N., & Payne, J. (2011). On the casual dynamics between renewable and non-renewable energy consumption and economic growth in developed and developing countries. *Energy Systems*, 2, 299–312.

Bellakhal, R., Ben Kheder, S., & Haffoudhi, H. (2019). Governance and renewable energy investment in MENA countries: How does trade matter? *Energy Economics*, 84, 1–15.

BP. (2020). Statistical Review of World Energy. Retrieved July 10, 2020, from http://www.bp.com/statisticalreview.

El Fadel, M., Rachid, G., El-Samra, R., Bou Boutros, G., & Hashisho, J. (2013). Emissions reduction and economic implications of renewable energy market penetration of power generation for residential consumption in the MENA region. *Energy Policy*, 52, 618–627.

EU. (2018). Directive (EU) 2018/2001 of the European Parliament and of the Council of 11 December 2018 on the promotion of the use of energy from renewable sources. Official Journal of the European Union, 82-210. Retrieved June 20, 2020, from EUR-Lex: https://eur-lex.europa.eu/legal-content/EN/TXT/?uri=uriserv:OJ.L_.2018.328.01.0082.01.ENG&toc=OJ:L:2018:328:TOC.

Farhani, S. (2013). Renewable energy consumption, economic growth and CO_2 emissions: Evidence from selected MENA countries. *Energy Economics Letters*, 1, 24–41.

Farzaneh, H., McLellan, B., & Ishihara, K. (2016). Toward a CO_2 zero emissions energy system in the Middle East region. *International Journal of Green Energy*, 13, 682–694.

Griffiths, S. (2017). A review and assessment of energy policy in the Middle East and North Africa region. *Energy Policy*, 102, 249–269.

IEA. (2020). Renewables Information: Overview. Retrieved July 25, 2020, from https://www.iea.org/reports/renewables-information-overview.

IMF. (2019). Regional Economic Outlook Update: Middle East, North Africa, Afghanistan, and Pakistan. International Monetary Fund. Retrieved June 30, 2020, from https://www.imf.org/en/Publications/REO/MECA/Issues/2019/04/17/reo-menap-cca-0419.

IRENA. (2019). Renewable Power Generation Costs in 2018. The International Renewable Energy Agency, Abu Dhabi. Retrieved July 20, 2020, from https://www.irena.org/publications/2019/May/Renewable-power-generation-costs-in-2018#RestrictedModal.

IRENA. (2020). Renewable Energy Statistics 2020. The International Renewable Energy Agency, Abu Dhabi. Retrieved July 10, 2020, from www.irena.org/Publications.

IRENA. (n.d.). IRENA RE Time Series. The International Renewable Energy Agency. Retrieved July 10, 2020, from https://public.tableau.com/views/IRENARETimeSeries/Charts?:embed=y&:showVizHome=no&publish=yes&:toolbar=no.

IRENA, & League of Arab States. (2014). Pan-Arab Renewable Energy Strategy 2030. Retrieved June 30, 2020, from https://www.irena.org/publications/2014/Jun/Pan-Arab-Renewable-Energy-Strategy-2030-Roadmap-of-Actions-for-Implementation.

Kahia, M., Ben Aïssa, M., & Lanouar, C. (2017). Renewable and non-renewable energy use-economic growth nexus: The case of MENA Net Oil Importing Countries. *Renewable and Sustainable Energy Reviews*, 71, 127–140.

Kahia, M., Ben Jebli, M., & Belloumi, M. (2019). Analysis of the impact of renewable energy consumption and economic growth on carbon dioxide emissions in 12 MENA countries. *Clean Technologies and Environmental Policy*, 21, 871–885.

Kitous, A., Saveyn, B., Keramidas, K., Vandyck, T., Rey Los Santos, L., & Wojtowicz, K. (2016). Impact of low oil prices on oil exporting countries. Publications office of the European Union. Retrieved June 25, 2020, from https://ec.europa.eu/jrc/en/publication/eur-scientific-and-technical-research-reports/impact-low-oil-prices-oil-exporting-countries#:~:text=The%20results%20show%20that%20such,Saharan%20Africa%20by%20around%208.5%25.

McGlade, C., & Ekins, P. (2015). The geographical distribution of fossil fuels unused when limiting global warming to 2 °C. *Nature*, 517, 187–190.

Pao, H., Li, Y., & Fu, H. (2014). Clean energy, non-clean energy, and economic growth in the MIST countries. *Energy Policy*, 67, 932–942.

Penna, A. N. (2020). *A History of Energy Flows: From Human Labor to Renewable Power*. New York: Routledge.

REN21. (2020). Renewables 2020 Global Status Report. Retrieved July 30, 2020, from https://www.ren21.net/wp-content/uploads/2019/05/gsr_2020_full_report_en.pdf.

statista. (2020). Retrieved July 15, 2020, from https://www.statista.com/statistics/267158/number-of-nuclear-reactors-in-operation-by-country/.

Trieb, F., Schillings, C., Pregger, T., & O'Sullivan, M. (2012). Solar electricity imports from the Middle East and North Africa to Europe. *Energy Policy*, 42, 341–353.

WDI. (n.d.). World Development Indicators. The World Bank. Retrieved July 20, 2020, from https://databank.worldbank.org/source/world-development-indicators.

Chapter 9

From Past to Future

The Entrepreneurial Ecosystem for Energy Start-ups in Turkey

Özlem Kunday

ABSTRACT

Energy has always been considered a valuable and critical resource by nations. Therefore, for many decades the control and management of this sector was executed by governmental institutions. With a paradigm shift in the 1980s, the trend of deregulation and privatization of public infrastructure in energy services starts to dominate the global arena. This chapter focuses on how the privatization and deregulations in the energy sector have opened opportunities for private companies and entrepreneurs in Turkey. After a short retrospective introduction on the journey of privatization at the macro level, a meso-level description of the development of private-sector energy companies is provided. Focus is on the micro level through a detailed review of the Turkish entrepreneurial ecosystem for start-ups in the energy sector. Here, several actors in the ecosystem are identified. Based on interviews with top-level managers of energy companies and nongovernmental organizations located in İstanbul, valuable insights are provided for entrepreneurs intending to enter the energy sector.

Keywords: Privatization, Energy Start-ups, Entrepreneurial Ecosystem

PRIVATIZATION OF THE ENERGY SECTOR IN TURKEY

Energy has always been considered a valuable and critical resource by nations. Therefore, for many decades the control and management of this sector was executed by governmental institutions (Popp et al., 2020). With a paradigm shift in the 1980s, the trend of deregulation and privatization of public infrastructure in energy services starts to be dominating the global arena. Deregulation efforts in the Turkish energy sector have been successfully carried out since 2002. New regulations and the establishment of the Energy Market Regulatory Authority (EPDK) during this period ensured that the process was managed in a healthy manner. By 2013, the state handed over all power plants to the private sector. Energy Markets Operating Corporation (EPİAŞ) was established; Energy Exchange Istanbul (EXIST) started operations. Undoubtedly, a radical change took place in the electricity sector with privatization. Thanks to heavy investment by the private sector in recent years, electricity shortages and blackouts have ended and excess supply began to occur. In addition, the quality of electricity and thus the safety of operators and efficiency of the process has increased. The Turkish energy sector is a tightly regulated one, with the Ministry of Energy and EPDK having a significant influence (www.tobb.org.tr). But there is still room to play.

DEVELOPMENT OF THE ENERGY SECTOR AND ROLE OF TURKISH PRIVATE ENERGY COMPANIES

Turkey is a net energy importer country. Approximately 77 percent of the total energy need is imported (tr.euronews.com). This confronts us with the main motivation factor to put in place domestic and renewable energy sources. Turkey's attempts to reduce dependence on foreign energy and national resources remain, keeping a busy agenda in its orientation. While localization continues to be one of the government's most fundamental policies in energy, efforts are made to pave the way for domestic technology investments, including areas such as renewable energy sources.

In fact, Turkey is a very rich country in terms of renewable energy sources. Especially in the last ten years, since the costs of renewable energy investments have decreased radically, significant developments have occurred in this area (TEPG1, 2018). As of 2019, 48 percent of the installed power and 43 percent of the electricity production was obtained from renewable energy sources. In this sense, Turkey has already gone beyond the targets set by many countries. Thanks to the government's incentives and supports in this field, investors' interest has always been high. Unlicensed and licensed electricity production and large-scale YEKA (Renewable Energy Resource Area) models have been developed and implemented by the government to promote renewable energy investments (www2.deloitte.com).

On the other hand, the government has kept the use of local resources in an important place among its energy supply policies. In particular, it has defined a tender method for utilizing domestic coal reserves with private-sector investments.

The natural gas sector also has an important place in Turkey. Since it is largely used for electricity production and heating of households, it is critical for the security of the energy supply. To secure this, natural gas storage facilities are being constructed.

Turkey is situated in a transit route between suppliers and large energy consumers. In this sense, it has a strategic position that serves as a regional energy hub (Saygin et al., 2018). Undoubtedly, Turkey's geopolitical importance is growing through existing and planned oil/gas pipelines.

Turkey's Nuclear Power Plant (NPP) journey began in 2010 with the agreement of Akkuyu NPP. Studies on Akkuyu NPP in the last two years have gained great speed. Sinop NPP project, another NPP planned to be built, was stopped in September 2019 due to the cost and timing matters.

While all these are discussed in the field of production in the energy sector, on the other hand, energy efficiency, which we can qualify as the cheapest, most environmentally friendly energy source, has an important place. In this regard, very important steps were taken after the energy efficiency law published in 2007. To summarize, the National Energy Efficiency Action Plan was published in 2018, and according to this plan, a total investment of $11 billion will be made by 2023, resulting in massive energy savings (enerji.gov.tr).

First, it should be said that Turkey is a fast-growing country with an average annual growth rate of 5.5 percent. Such a growth rate has not been observed in any OECD country since 2002. When the population growth is added to this, the need for energy resources is in a rapid increase. By the end of 2018, the country's primary energy supply doubled. Considering the investments to be made by the private sector to meet the increasing need, the total installed power is expected to reach 110 GW in 2023 (sbb.gov.tr).

Considering the current situation of Turkey's energy sector, with its strategic location in the energy distribution, renewable energy and energy efficiency potential, having established the long-term business partnerships for natural gas distribution, can be listed as strengths. On the other hand, economic fluctuations, the low level of R&D studies compared to the world average, and investor dissatisfaction in the energy distribution and marketing activities can be counted as weak spots.

Besides, there are some opportunities in the market: such as the flow of energy from the West to the East; renewable energy production is open to development; and investors are in appetite for energy storage and other technologies. For the risks in the market, geopolitical risks, fluctuations in exchange rates, and high level of foreign dependency on energy resources can be said.

There are huge companies operating in the energy sector, as well as many small- and medium-size enterprises. The majority in the value chain activities are private-sector companies. According to data released in 2020, among Turkey's top 100 companies, an energy company named TÜPRAŞ was the first in the ranking (www.iso500.org). Furthermore, there are four energy sector companies in the top 20 and 14 in the top 100. While large companies implement corporate management strategies, small- and medium-size enterprises need to improve their institutional capacities. Energy is a commodity that is transferred through various parties until it reaches its end users.

Industry 4.0 brings together technologies that lead to unprecedented paradigm shifts in the economy for business, society, and individuals. According to experts and executives in the energy industry, three basic trends emerge as a result of this transformation process. The future in the energy sector will be shaped around these three trends, and we will experience the game-changing effects of this transformation.

One of these trends is electrification, which means electricity will enter our lives more. Electricity demand will increase by 80 percent in the next twenty-five years. The main triggering factors of this change are transportation and heating.

The second trend is decentralization resulting from a sharp drop in the costs of distributed energy sources such as distributed production, distributed storage, demand response, and energy efficiency.

The third trend is digitalization. There, the main drivers will be the digitalization of the network with the use of smart metering, smart sensors, automation, and other digital technologies. In addition to these, the dramatic increase in the number of devices connected with the Internet of Things will result in an enormous growth of the size of network users.

It is expected that in this new world, the role of distribution companies will go far beyond delivering electricity to the end user, just like GSM operators are in the process of changing service. In this new process, distribution companies will serve as a platform to maximize the benefits of distributed energy sources. The revenue generation model will change. The income source that is traditionally about electricity distribution will shrink, but this will be compensated by new distribution and retail services.

This new system, namely, more distributed, more connected, and smarter grid structure, will improve energy availability, increase supply security, minimize environmental impacts, and perhaps increase the utilization of network investments and existing capacity as a crucial element, and new business models will create new business opportunities.

According to the latest assessment by the World Economic Forum, electricity transformation will create a value of more than $2.4 trillion over the next ten years. New technologies will provide new opportunities for employment, consumers will have more choices, and access to clean energy resources of the society will increase.

The demand for energy is increasing due to urbanization, industrialization, and digitalization. According to the IEA forecast, this increase will be 40 percent in 2050 (www.iea.org). But the need for electricity will increase twice the amount. The first reason is that the loads for heating purposes will turn to electricity, and the second is transportation. There are different assumptions about how fast electric vehicles will be included in our lives. This will provide progress in autonomous driving technology and storage technologies. Autonomous cars will come and bring us extra comfort, efficiency, and safety. The vehicles will be a new workspace, reading area, entertainment area, and even a sleeping area for us.

A second main trend observed is that distributed energy sources will enter our lives. At the moment, users' interest in electricity is only a few minutes to take a look at the electricity bill that comes out every month. This will not happen in the world of tomorrow. The end user will go from passive to active. Progress in renewable energy technologies and a decrease in costs will trigger this. Users will switch to producer status. They will use as much as they need, store the rest, and sell at the right time. This sales process will take place thanks to autonomous smart systems. A smart thermostat we use in our home will learn our habits and preferences over time and make its own program. It will automatically stop the heating/cooling system when an attractive price proposal comes from the network at a time when the energy need is high. It will sell the stored energy to the grid.

Energy efficiency is a subcomponent of distributed energy. According to IEA estimates, every penny spent on energy efficiency prevents at least twice as much new investment cost (www.iea.org). When we consider our foreign dependency status in energy, it will become a subject we attach more importance to in the future.

DEMAND SIDE MANAGEMENT OR DEMAND RESPONSE IS ANOTHER SUBCOMPONENT OF DISTRIBUTED ENERGY

Depending on population growth and increased revenues referring to Turkey, we see that the primary energy consumption increased rapidly. Turkey ranks second after China in the increase in energy demand. The annual electricity consumption increase rate of the country has been above 5 percent in the last fifteen years. The renewable energy and energy efficiency potential is huge, and the government is very keen on unlocking this potential.

Especially the size of the renewable energy market creates an opportunity for local companies to do R&D and improve their technologies. The support given by the government to domestic production increases this possibility.

According to Turkey's 2023 vision, $22 billion in wind energy, $27 billion in nuclear energy, $7 billion in solar, $14 billion in coal, $17 billion in Hydro, $15 billion in grid infrastructure are planned to be invested (www.setav.org).

While all these create a competitive advantage, the inadequacy of innovation and the ongoing dependence in this area constitute a weakness. Turkey, to reduce its energy intensity and to achieve a competitive advantage, instead of low added value, energy-intensive, and old technology industrial sectors, should give priority to high-tech industry and domestic production.

ENTREPRENEURIAL ECOSYSTEM FOR ENERGY START-UPS IN TURKEY

The concept of the ecosystem is being used in many disciplines to describe the environment required for new livings to flourish. Within the entrepreneurship context, we define an entrepreneurial ecosystem as a system of nexus among independent yet interdependent actors in a certain geographical region that together create a favorable and encouraging environment in which new ventures can blossom. According to Isenberg (2010), the conditions that define the infrastructure of an entrepreneurial ecosystem can be listed as the availability of financial capital, governmental support, success stories, societal norms, nongovernmental organizations (NGOs), support professionals, infrastructure, educational institutions, labor, networks, early customers, and leadership.

The Turkish entrepreneurial ecosystem is a continuously growing one. This can be observed by the number of new actors entering the system each year as well as by the results of academic studies. One of the most important studies on this topic is the Global Entrepreneurship Monitor (GEM) study. The results of the Global Entrepreneurship Monitor study imply that between the years 2016 and 2018, there is a clear favorable improvement measured in the infrastructure of the elements that determine the Turkish Entrepreneurship ecosystem (www.yuvam.yeditepe.edu.tr).

More recent data shows that even under the negative circumstances created by the COVID-19 pandemic period during the second quarter of 2020, the investments from business angels and VCs in start-ups have increased by 44 percent when compared with the preceding quarter. Again, in the second quarter of 2020, twenty-eight start-ups from Turkey have received a total of $29 million investment. So far it can be concluded that COVID-19 has not yet shown a negative effect on the investments in start-ups (www.startups.watch). As stated earlier, the energy industry is the one in which capital-related costs play an important role.

Whether fossil fuel plants, nuclear plants, or renewable technologies, all of them are capital intensive. In Turkey, the R&D activities of companies operating in the energy sector are supported significantly. These supports are mostly provided by the Ministry of Science, Industry and Technology. Technology investments, especially for producing high added value products, are among the top priorities of the government.

Turkey, according to the European Innovation Scoreboard 2019, is a "Moderate Innovator" country (www.ec.europa.eu). Non-R&D innovation expenditures, SMEs innovating in-house, and SMEs with marketing or organizational innovations are the areas where the country is performing well. Technology development centers and universities play an important role in this field. Examples of this exist in Turkey. For example, Enerjisa supports innovation projects in cooperation with ITU Early Stage Incubation Center. It becomes a strong partner, mentor, and sponsor at every stage of innovation (www.enerjisa.com).

In terms of suppliers of the energy sector, it can be said that it is easy to access the qualified global and local companies in related fields. Two important corporate actors within the ecosystem are Enerjisa and Limak Energy. Both of them have been active players within the Turkish energy sector since the beginning of the privatization started by means of several huge investments they made as private-sector corporations. Now, they are also pioneering with their corporate entrepreneurship and accelerator programs for energy start-ups.

Enerjisa prioritizes support to energy start-ups that are following the trends of digitalization, sustainability, and efficiency. They will continue to exist as an active actor that supports start-ups within this space as well as corporate entrepreneurship via their entrepreneurship platform named "NAR." NAR was launched in 2015 based on their strong belief in corporate entrepreneurship as an investment devoted to foster an innovative corporate culture. Thus, as Enerjisa they support corporate projects, that is, intrapreneurs, that will generate more than 50 million TL value with the innovative business models they offer in digitalization and innovation. Empowered by incentives and motivational support mechanisms, the primary purpose of our corporate entrepreneurship program is to unite with our employee in our shared corporate goals and thereby produce dynamism and energy.

Furthermore, they are in the opinion that technology-related innovation comes from innovative start-ups. Therefore, they also collaborate with and support start-ups outside of their corporation. At Enerjisa NAR, they are very much aware that corporate entrepreneurship programs are contemporary applications that foster new ideas to arise and trigger innovation. Consequently, they approach and evaluate new ideas coming from their employees as a potential start-up which results in terrific internal dynamism.

Innovative business models or those that develop new product or services and add new digital competencies to the company are supported by agile management styles and pilot applications. To further support the digital competencies and awareness of their employees, they continue to offer them training in their in-house Digital Academy (www.enerjisa.com).

TEA (Turkish Energy Academy) was initiated in 2018 by Limak Energy as an Energy Start-up Accelerator Program with the vision to adjust to the fast-changing demands of the energy sector. Limak, just as Enerjisa, is another Pioneer acting both as a private-sector energy provider and an actor supporting new energy start-ups. This program is the very first accelerator program in the Turkish entrepreneurial ecosystem that focuses only on energy start-ups and, therefore, a very important actor.

TEA Limak Energy Start-up Accelerator Program offers a unique opportunity for a wide range of parties such as energy start-ups, entrepreneurs, as well as potential entrepreneurs. They provide their participants access to their mentors and open up their valuable resources such as know-how, experience, access to market, networking and many more. The mentoring part is carried out by the Mentors Network Turkey, whereas the sector experience sharing part by Limak Energy mentors (turkiyeninenerjiakademi si.com).

With the help of this rich blend and combination of support, participants can develop new business ideas, innovative business models, and new technologies needed in the energy sector. They believe that start-ups can be initiated and grown with the support of an effective entrepreneurial ecosystem in place (medium.com).

ERA OF START-UPS IN THE TURKISH ENERGY SECTOR

Energy start-ups will be important role players in the growing modular technologies and in grid integration by offering high-tech solutions within a still capital intensive industry.

Most of the energy start-ups have to adapt a B2B business model. Since last year, there has been a new tendency and working with start-ups has become popular conduct. This has been initiated by the Turkish Ministry for Energy and Natural resources toward closer cooperation with start-ups.

Energy efficiency offers many opportunities for innovative Turkish start-ups. This sector has been emphasized particularly by the ministry of energy to be approached by start-ups.

These start-ups are to exist in wind, solar, and nuclear energy areas. The main purpose here is to diminish Turkey's dependency on imported products to be used in energy-related issues. It has been stated that there will be an obligation for all pieces to be produced in Turkey that are going to be used for the transformation of all lamps to LED ones that are used in cities. There will also be financial support available for local producers (medium .com).

Companies often need alliances and partnerships with other companies to create added value for their customers and gain a competitive advantage. Building strong, related, and supportive industries that help domestic companies compete globally can take a long time and need a lot of investment. But this is necessary to gain a long-term competitive advantage.

According to the opinion of experts, the market mechanism for energy demand side management will be introduced soon. The aim of this mechanism is to manage the demand level at the peak hours of the day and the level of distributed production and storage that will meet this demand. For this, it is necessary to automatically generate signals with quantity and price information, and sometimes to offer attractive financial offers. This need in the market opens a space for start-ups to tap in.

The effects of the digitalization trend will continue to be effective. IoT, artificial intelligence technologies, and data analytics will increase their impact on all trends in the coming period. With digitalization, efficiency will come first. In Turkey, we have 40–50 percent efficiency potential in buildings and 20–30 percent in industry, and it is not possible to realize this potential without using IoT-based technologies because this does not happen by removing barriers to heating, not even by installing an automation system. It is with a system where the smart room thermostat learns your comfort needs over time and reaches real-time weather forecast data and regulates the room temperature.

Process efficiency will come. Improvement will be made up to 60 percent in investment costs and 75 percent in operating costs. How will this happen: engineering and commissioning costs will be reduced, digital twin concept will change our lives, and maintenance costs will decrease. Instead of reactive maintenance when the malfunction occurs, analytics that will allow preventive and predictive maintenance will be used. Planned periodic stops will no longer be required because the software will inform which critical equipment will cause problems when. Thus, production continuity will be ensured. The life of the assets will increase, and its performance will improve.

The availability and quality of energy will be guaranteed. The safety of the user regarding the use of electricity will be further improved: sensors and software will be able to predict malfunctions. Alarm analytics will enable this. Augmented reality will both provide operator security and facilitate access to information.

Our carbon footprint will decrease because the software will decide when we need to use the energy we produce from our network. It will enable us to manage a bilateral flow of energy as the demand side. When the network says I need energy, it will say I can give it wisely. Instead of establishing a new power plant, it will ensure optimum utilization of the existing capacity.

The more difficult the domestic market demands are for the countries, the better the companies of that country are prepared for the future. It creates a significant competitive advantage for foreign market conditions because the challenging conditions make those companies more innovative, qualified, and flexible.

NGO'S IN THE TURKISH ENERGY SECTOR: THE CASE OF EYODER (ENERGY EFFICIENCY AND MANAGEMENT ASSOCIATION)

To get more insight information on the role and purpose of NGOs in the Turkish energy sector, an interview with Cihan Karamık was conducted. Cihan Karamık is an electrical engineer and actively served for more than twenty years at different managerial positions within the Turkish energy sector. His last position as a top-level manager was at a Global Energy Company's Office in Istanbul.

Mr. Cihan Karamık has started by emphasizing that "*as EYODER* (Energy Efficiency and Management Association) members, we are energy optimists. We think that it is possible to find a solution to this dilemma that we live in using today's technologies. For this, we only need to switch from the culture of consuming energy to managing."

In this context, when the discussions in the energy world are observed, he mentioned that we often see people talking about alternatives on the supply side such as nuclear and other options, shale gas and options, fossil fuels, and renewable energy sources. However, there is another rapidly growing school of thought: the belief that real priority is in energy efficiency. EYODER state that they are the representatives of this school. They know that the easiest, cheapest, fastest, and most profitable way to produce green energy is to use and manage energy smarter.

According to the data of the International Energy Agency, 58 percent of the energy efficiency potential in the industry, 79 percent of the efficiency potential in the infrastructure sector, and 82 percent of the potential in the buildings have never been touched. If these potentials can be realized in terms of energy efficiency, we can fight climate change more easily and become more hopeful for a sustainable world.

Mr. Karamık states that "As EYODER, we set off in May 2010 to keep this hope alive for our country. Our aim was to bring together Energy Efficiency Consultancy (EVD) companies and professionals working in the field of energy efficiency and management under a Civil Society Organization to contribute to the development of the Energy Efficiency (EV) sector in our country."

Energy Efficiency and Management Association (EYODER) has worked for the healthy development of the energy efficiency sector since its establishment. EYODER has gathered energy efficiency consultancy companies, energy managers, and other related sectoral associations, institutions, banks, and manufacturers, and implementing companies on many platforms in order to fulfill the duties specified in the law in buildings and industrial facilities.

The association argues that it is imperative to "manage" energy all the time in order to reveal the real power of the sector and to provide unity of power. In this sense, it supported many works carried out in public and private sectors with active participation.

There are currently forty-five EVD companies listed on the website of the Energy Efficiency and Environmental Management Department (EVÇED). Three of them have authority in the field of education, fourteen in the industry sector, thirty-nine in the building sector, and eight in both industry and building sectors. Twenty-one of these companies are members of our association. In addition to EVD companies, they also have members from suppliers working in the field of energy efficiency, energy efficiency experts, and university representatives working in institutions and organizations. This diversity is also reflected in their management board. Their claim is to make very important contributions to the energy efficiency sector and our country by making good use of the synergy created by this diversity.

The EVD members of EYODER basically uncover efficiency potentials by conducting energy studies in buildings and industry. They prepare efficiency-enhancing project files for businesses and enable businesses to receive grants from the government. They provide consultancy services to businesses related to energy efficiency and ISO50001 energy management. They issue an Energy Identity document for existing buildings. They provide testing, measurement, and commissioning services.

However, many of their EVD members have started a serious transformation process toward becoming "ESCO" (Energy Service Company). In the ESCO business model, there is an understanding of realizing energy efficiency projects with "energy performance contracts" and guaranteeing savings performance, thereby minimizing the risks of investors who want to develop projects. Thanks to this model, which has been applied for many years, especially in Europe and the United States, it is possible to realize the potential of untouched energy efficiency. In this business model, it is easier to progress in projects with limited scope and certain limits. The development of measurement and verification legislation is also essential for the resolution of possible disputes. In this direction, legal infrastructure has been established in our country and secondary legislation studies are also continuing.

EYODER carries out EU projects in cooperation with other NGOs and universities to create added value in line with the needs of the energy efficiency sector, while trying to draw attention to energy efficiency; for example, they are about to complete.

A European Union project that was one among the thirty-eight projects that were accepted between 500 filed applications. The project titled "Improving the Communication and Data Sharing Network among Energy Efficiency Stakeholders" is aimed to strengthen the capacity and improve administrative, advocacy, and communication skills for EYODER's more active and democratic participation in policymaking and decision-making processes. In addition, another goal is to establish a "Database" on Energy Efficiency and to increase communication among stakeholders.

CONCLUSION AND FUTURE DIRECTIONS

The Turkish energy sector consists of mainly private-sector companies. The role of government is more of a supporting, policy developing and thereby guiding and facilitating one. On the other hand, energy is a commodity that passes through various stages until it reaches the final consumers. With the transformations and changing trends, companies need to anticipate and develop their strategies on what type of future they will be facing. Accordingly, new, innovative business models and altered positioning actions need to be delivered. The Industry 4.0 related advancements in the energy sector triggered by data analytics, AI, and IoT created new spaces of opportunities for Turkish academicians, Corporations, start-ups, and all interested parties to emphasize. Instead of big and integrated organizational structures, we observe more dispersed and more agile, smaller business entering the arena. This distributed nature of the energy value chain activities allows several actors to become participants, and the expectation is that the number of stakeholders will increase.

The increase in innovative technology-related energy start-ups will also enable investors to direct their investments to these projects. There already exists a pool of government-initiated funds available. However, it needs to be enriched. By adding more creative financial resources such as crowdfunding could certainly be beneficial. At each point of the energy value chain activities, there is a need for financing to market the resource flow possible.

To conclude, it can be observed that there are many professionals within governmental institutions, NGOs, and the private sector that are eager to collaborate with start-ups. With more support and the right actors in the ecosystem, there is a high potential for success stories and further unicorns to come from Turkey.

REFERENCES

Ayvacı, Ö. A. (2019). Ziya Erdem: 50 milyon tl'yi aşan değer yaratıyoruz. https://startup.capital.com.tr/soylesi/ziya-erdem-50-milyon-tlyi-asan-deger-yaratiyoruz.html retrieved on 01.06.2020.

Deloitte (2021). YEKA: Yenilenebilir Enerji Kaynak Alanı. https://www2.deloitte.com/tr/tr/pages/energy-and-resources/articles/yenilenebilir-enerji-kaynak-alani.html.

Dünya Enerji Konseyi Türkiye (2018). Türkiye Enerji Piyasaları Araştırma Raporu. https://www.dunyaenerji.org.tr/wp-content/uploads/2018/07/TEPG1.pdf. https://enerjiapi.etkb.gov.tr//Media/Dizin/EVCED/Raporlar/Ulusal%20%Verimliliği%20Eylem%20Planı/20180102M1_2018_eng.pdf retrieved on 01.07.2020.

Euronews (2019) Türkiye, 39 Avrupa ülkesi içinde enerjide ithalat en fazla bağımlı beşinci ülke. https://tr.euronews.com/2019/08/29/turkiye-39-avrupa-ulkesi-icinde-enerjide-ithalata-en-fazla-bagimli-besinci-ulke retrieved on 19.07.2020.

EYODER (2017) Uusal Enerji Verimliliği Eylem Planı 2017-2023 http://www.eyo-der.org.tr/UlusalEVEP.pdf retrieved on 28.03.2021

IEA (2020). World Energy Outlook. https://www.iea.org/topics/world-energy-outlook retrieved on 08.07.2020.

Isenberg, D. J. (2010). How to start an entrepreneurial revolution. *Harvard Business Review*, *88*(6), 40–50.

İstanbul Sanayı Odası (2019) 2019 yılı Türkiye'nin 500Büyük Sanayi Kuruluşu. http://www.iso500.org.tr retrieved on 03.08.2020.

Kavaz, İ. (2019). Türkiye'nin Enerjide Gelecek Vizyonu.

Limak Enerji (2018). TEA İnovasyon programı. https://www.turkiyeninenerjiakademisi.com/program-hakkinda retrieved on 08.06.2020.

Ocakoğlu, Ö.O. and Altun, F. (2017) Müşteri Deneyiminde Oyun Kurucu Olacağız. https://www.enerjisa.com.tr/tr/enerjisa-hakkinda/medya-merkezi/basin-bultenleri/90 retrieved on 09.07.202.

Orbay, B. (2019). Enerji Startupları Türkiye'nin Sonraki Başarı Hikayesi mi? https://medium.com/@berk.orbay/enerji-startupları-türkiyenin-sonraki-başarı-hikayesi-mi-de7d84f1fd95 retrieved on 07.07.2020.

Popp, D., Pless, J., Haščič, I., & Johnstone, N. (2020). *Innovation and Entrepreneurship in the Energy Sector* (No. w27145). National Bureau of Economic Research.

Saygin, D., Hoffman, M., & Godron, P. (2018). How Turkey Can Ensure a Successful Energy Transition. *SHURA Energy Transition Centre, Centre for American Progress, Agora Energiewende, Istanbul, Washington, DC, Berlin.*

TOBB (2015) VIII. Türkiye Sektörel Ekonomi Şurası https://www.tobb.org.tr/Documents/yayinlar/2015/8Sektorel-Ekonomi-Surasi.pdf retrieved on 08.07.2020.

Türkiye Sınai Kalkınma Bankası (2018) Sektörel Görünüm: Enerji. https://www.tskb.com.tr/i/assets/document/pdf/enerji-sektorel-gorunumu.pdf retrieved on 01.06.2020.

YUVAM (2019) Girişimcilik Raporu http://yuvam.yeditepe.edu.tr/pdf/girisimcilik_raporu_2019.pdfhttp://yuvam.yeditepe.edu.tr/pdf/girisimcilik_raporu_2019.pdf

Chapter 10

Sustainable Energy Supply Chain Management

Özlem Şenvar

ABSTRACT

Energy supply has become one of the world's major issues. Energy resources are necessary for industrial power processes. For efficient and effective supply chains, concepts of sustainable energy supply chain management are required to be taken into considerations for the conditions to improve the usage and accessibility of energy. Supply chain trends influence the energy industries. From this standpoint, this chapter presents a conceptual overview of sustainable energy supply chain management. In this regard, the fundamental aim of this chapter is to present a conceptual overview of supply chain management, sustainable supply chain management, energy supply chain management, and sustainable energy supply chain management. Discussion and recommendations for the future of sustainable energy supply chain management are emphasized, as well.

Keywords: Supply Chain Management; Energy Management; Sustainability

INTRODUCTION

Energy resources are vital to industrial power processes. In this regard, for efficient and effective supply chains, concepts of sustainable energy supply chain management are required to be taken into considerations for the conditions to improve the usage and accessibility of energy (Halldórsson & Svanberg, 2013).

Notably, global supply chains are facing risks of energy shortages. Hence, policy makers of companies as well as countries must increase their levels of awareness of the vulnerability of their supply chains for energy management. Currently, it has become inevitable to minimize risks of uncertainties arisen from unforeseeable situations and maximize stability within the global energy supply chains.

There are potential benefits, which are listed below, make renewables an attractive option for the supply chain:

- Avoiding risks of fossil fuel price fluctuations and regulatory changes
- Attract customers, partners, and employees interested in corporate responsibility
- Drive corporate growth by keeping pace with competitors
- Switching to renewables selectively or throughout the supply chain can help decrease long-term costs, provide price stability, mitigate future regulatory risk, enhance brand value, drive new revenue, and improve employee engagement

This chapter aims to provide a conceptual overview of sustainable energy supply chain management. The rest of this chapter is organized as follows: In Section 'Supply Chain Management', the concepts of supply chain management is explained. Section 'Sustainable Supply Chain Management' gives sustainable supply chain management concepts. Section 'Energy Supply Chain Management' summarizes energy supply chain management. Section 'Sustainable Energy Supply Chain Management' involves a conceptual overview of sustainable energy supply chain management. The last section presents the conclusion and provides insights into the future of supply chain management. Moreover, further directions for sustainable energy supply chain management are emphasized in this section.

SUPPLY CHAIN MANAGEMENT

The supply chain is also known as a value chain. Value refers to the relative usefulness of an object. In the case of a product or business, value defines the relative benefit of acquiring a product or of the existence of a particular business (Loucopoulos & Karakostas, 1995).

The supply chain has a complex structure due to the fact that it is characterized by numerous activities spread over multiple functions and organizations, which pose interesting challenges for effective supply chain coordination (Kanda & Deshmukh, 2008). Principally, the supply chain is considered as a network in which a company and its suppliers produces and distributes a specific product or service for customers. This network covers different processes along with activities with people, entities, information, raw materials, and energy resources. Mentzer et al. (2001) defined the supply chain as a set of three or more entities (organizations or individuals) directly involved in the upstream and downstream flows of products, services, finances, and/or information from a source to a customer. It has to be emphasized that the supply chain involves different actors for a product throughout its life cycle. As a matter of fact, the optimized supply chain is vital to satisfy customer requirements.

Porter (2011) developed a supply or value chain that links all stakeholders to satisfy customers' requirements. The value identification of customers and stakeholders determines a business strategy and target profit performance.

Effective development and management of the supply chain network will enhance the minimization of costs and maximization of customer value. Hence, as its name implies, supply chain management is the management of the flow of goods and services and includes all processes that transform raw materials into final products. Mentzer et al. (2001) defined supply chain management as the systemic, strategic coordination of the traditional business functions and the tactics across these business functions within a particular company and across businesses within the supply chain, for the purposes of improving the long-term performance of the individual companies and the supply chain as a whole. In other words, supply chain management considers streamlining of supply-side activities to maximize customer value and maintaining competitiveness. The Council of Supply Chain Management Professionals (CSCMP) defines logistics management as part of supply chain management that plans, implements, and controls the efficient, effective forward and reverses flow and storage of goods, services and related information between the point of origin and the point of consumption in order to satisfy customers' requirements.

Logistics management and supply chain management have been traditionally associated with inventory management, forecasting, transportation, and network optimization (Fontes & Freires, 2018). Marchi and Zanoni (2017) listed the key aspects of supply chain management as follows:

- Distribution network configuration
- Inventory control
- Supply contracts
- Distribution strategies
- Supply chain integration and strategic partnering
- Outsourcing and procurement strategies
- Information technology and decision support systems
- Consumer value

SUSTAINABLE SUPPLY CHAIN MANAGEMENT

As a matter of fact, the definition of sustainable supply chain management is wider than traditional supply chain management. As its name implies, sustainable supply chain management merges sustainability and supply chain management.

Globalization is imposing supply chain management to extend pure economic issues like fair labor conditions and environmentally friendly production. This attitude raises interest in its intersection with sustainable development, which is usually comprehended in terms of economic, environmental, and social dimensions. From a broader perspective, organizational sustainability involves three dimensions, which are known as economic, environmental, and social. Managing supply chains in a sustainable manner has become an increasing concern for organizations or companies of all sizes and across a wide range of industries. Companies are responsible for responding to external pressure from governments, consumers, and nongovernmental organizations (NGOs), and media can be complemented by the development and introduction of sustainable products. Sustainable supply chain management is defined as the management of material, information, and capital flows, as well as cooperation among companies along the supply chain considering goals of three sustainable development dimensions (economic, environmental, and social) derived from customer and stakeholder requirements. In sustainable supply chains, environmental and social criteria need to be satisfied by the members to remain within the supply chain, while it is expected that competitiveness would be maintained through meeting customer needs and related economic criteria (Seuring & Müller, 2008a, 2008b).

Sustainable supply chain management identifies the environmental and social initiatives that can have the greatest economic impact. According to Porter and Kramer (2006); across the primary activities of the supply chain, inbound and outbound logistics activities can be distinguished as packaging use and disposal, warehouse safety, and transportation impacts such as emissions and safety; operations issues including emissions, energy use, hazardous materials, and worker safety and human rights; and after-sales service concerns comprising reverse logistics issues centering on environmentally sound disposal and disposition. It is evident that the environmental dimension clearly dominates, and social aspects are widely ignored or interpreted in an unusual manner (Seuring, 2013).

It has to be emphasized that sustainable supply chain management also covers green supply chain management. In sustainable supply chain management, there are two fundamental objectives, which are the performance assessment and the integration of the operations associated with environmental, social, and economic issues (Seuring & Müller, 2008a; Seuring, 2013; Hassini, 2012).

ENERGY SUPPLY CHAIN MANAGEMENT

The energy industry is experiencing complex global growth and other associated challenges such as aging infrastructures, complex and interdependent systems, increasing regulatory controls, and higher consumer expectations. There is pressure to increase supply chain productivity and profitability while facing these tough challenges. It is possible to say that supply chain trends influence the energy industries.

Principally, energy products delivered to the consumers are a result of the joint efforts of many organizations. All of these efforts comprise the supply chain. While the supply chain has been operating for many years, only organizations with physically existing facilities have come to the front.

Energy supply has become one of the world's major issues, and it has been examined with traditional methods to energy supply networks. In fact, the energy supply chain is the most functional stage of the supply chain that aims to increase customer's value and maintain a sustainable competitive advantage. The process of the supply chain includes all operations such as product development, supply, production, distribution, and a data system that organizes other operations. Eventually, information sharing supports many organizations in the supply chain to manage and schedule their operations and also to organize the product flow both for up and down the supply chain. There should be a connection between organizations in the supply chain in the form of both physical bonds and information sharing. These physical bonds include the transformation operations and warehousing of products and materials.

The energy chain can be defined as the trajectory of energy transformations from the fuel source or energy sources to useful energy form to end users. The production of fuels, heat, and electricity from different sources is defined by the appropriate energy supply chain.

SUSTAINABLE ENERGY SUPPLY CHAIN MANAGEMENT

As a matter of fact, renewable energy has become a driving force in the effort to sustain the earth's natural resources and to improve the users' quality of life. Renewable energy can be defined as a free source of sustainable energy, having no negative impacts during the conversion process like the emission of hazardous substances. Renewable energy has been an important issue in the green economy.

The use of fossil fuels causes harmful influences with greenhouse gas emissions to the environment, and the reserves of fossil fuels are limited. Hence, many countries have set goals for the development of renewable energy, specifically for its efficient generation and conversion to a consumable form of energy and its commercialization in the market. For the energy production process, it is necessary to evaluate the process in terms of both quantity and quality. For that reason, the energy and exergy efficiencies of an energy production process have to be taken into account: higher conversion costs, limited locations, environmental impacts, and other factors exposure barriers. In order to overcome these barriers, governments, researchers, and stakeholders should work together to enhance the conversion efficiency of renewable energy, develop advanced storage technologies, control distribution efficiency, and commercialize the use of renewable energy ultimately (Wee et al., 2012). In this regard, renewable energy, along with sustainable supply chain management, should be considered together. In other words, renewable energy and sustainable supply chain management play an important role in the global energy industry (Fontes & Freires, 2018).

Similar to a typical supply chain, the components of the renewable energy supply chain include the physical, information, and financial flows. From a physical flow perspective, industries increasing awareness of green manufacturing processes, logistics, and products has become relevant to its supply chain management performance (Wee et al., 2012).

New technologies are presenting promising opportunities for improvements across the supply chain, including innovations in renewable energy resources. Thus, in the renewable energy supply chain, technology is a key success factor to improve efficiency and to innovate the distribution network. In terms of demand, the commercialization of renewable energy would be an important step to replace traditional fossil energy. Efficient renewable energy generator and storage technologies are the crucial innovations for renewable energy.

The renewable energy supply chain consists of many stakeholders with different roles. Figure 10.1 shows the stakeholders and values of renewable energy in the supply chain (Evans, Strezov, & Evans, 2009; Menz & Vachon, 2006; Del Río & Burguillo, 2008). Notably, as it is explained in section "Supply Chain Management," the value identification of customers and stakeholders determines a business strategy and target profit performance. A sustainable supply chain must involve coordination among resources, flows, and stocks with a well-defined sustainability concept, and this requires more attention by all actors involved in the renewable energy supply chain.

From a holistic perspective, every single energy supply chain can be uniquely defined by several sustainability criteria. The sustainability criteria for the energy supply chain can be listed as follows: total energy efficiency of production, total exergy efficiency of an overall chain, the coefficient of exergy quality for different products at energy chains, economy of production, investment and environmental.

The optimal sustainable energy supply chain can be selected by using multicriteria optimization, which satisfies the above-mentioned sustainability

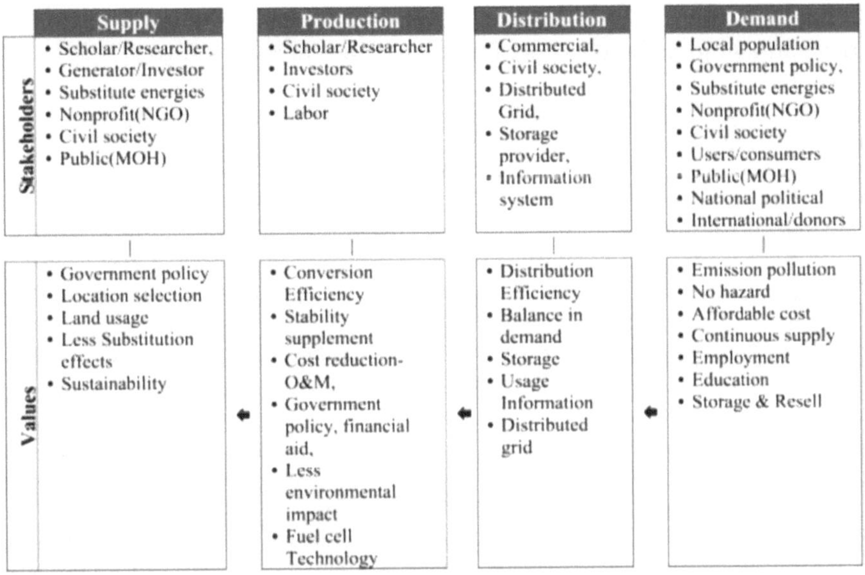

Figure 10.1 The stakeholders and the values of renewable energy supply chain. *Source*: (Evans, Strezov, & Evans, 2009; Menz & Vachon, 2006; Del Río & Burguillo, 2008).

criteria. This selected energy chain is close to an ideal solution. The ideal sustainable energy supply chain is formed from the set of energy production ways which are defined according to the sustainability criteria and which have a connection with the current status of technologies, economic, environmental and social parameters, and so on (Vasković et al., 2016).

CONCLUSION

Since sustainability is a target for sustainable development, more emphasis on the social aspect along with the environmental and economic aspects should be considered and involved in the sustainable energy supply chain management.

For the future of sustainable energy supply chain management, economic, environmental, and social issues should be examined via in-depth analyses across the supply chains. Lack of economic interventions and technological breakthroughs have significant effects on the growth of the energy industries.

The realization of renewable energy values, along with the improvement of distribution networks, and the development of advanced storage technologies are challenges for the development of sustainable energy supply chains. The technology and energy transition development requires innovative freight transport and logistics concepts for short-term efficiency gains.

REFERENCES

Chiaroni, D., Chiesa, M., Chiesa, V., Cucchiella, F., D'Adamo, I., & Frattini, F. (2015). An analysis of supply chains in renewable energy industries: A survey in Italy. In *Sustainable future energy technology and supply chains* (pp. 47–71). Springer, Cham.

CSCMP (Council of Supply Chain Management Professionals) (2013). CSCMP Supply Chain Management Definitions [Online]. Available at: http://cscmp.org/aboutcscmp/definitions.asp.

Del Río, P., & Burguillo, M. (2008). Assessing the impact of renewable energy deployment on local sustainability: Towards a theoretical framework. *Renewable and Sustainable Energy Reviews*, 12(5), 1325–1344.

Evans, A., Strezov, V., & Evans, T. J. (2009). Assessment of sustainability indicators for renewable energy technologies. *Renewable and Sustainable Energy Reviews*, 13(5), 1082–1088.

Fontes, C. H. D. O., & Freires, F. G. M. (2018). Sustainable and renewable energy supply chain: A system dynamics overview. *Renewable and Sustainable Energy Reviews*, 82, 247–259.

Halldórsson, Á., & Svanberg, M. (2013). Energy resources: trajectories for supply chain management. *Supply Chain Management: An International Journal.*

Hassini, E., Surti, C., & Searcy, C. (2012). A literature review and a case study of sustainable supply chains with a focus on metrics. *International Journal of Production Economics*, 140(1), 69–82.

Kanda, A., & Deshmukh, S. G. (2008). Supply chain coordination: perspectives, empirical studies and research directions. *International Journal of Production Economics*, 115(2), 316–335.

Loucopoulos, P., & Karakostas, V. (1995). *System requirements engineering.* McGraw-Hill, Inc.

Marchi, B., & Zanoni, S. (2017). Supply chain management for improved energy efficiency: Review and opportunities. *Energies*, 10(10), 1618.

Mentzer, J. T., DeWitt, W., Keebler, J. S., Min, S., Nix, N. W., Smith, C. D., & Zacharia, Z. G. (2001). Defining supply chain management. *Journal of Business Logistics*, 22(2), 1–25.

Menz, F. C., & Vachon, S. (2006). The effectiveness of different policy regimes for promoting wind power: Experiences from the states. *Energy Policy*, 34(14), 1786–1796.

Porter, M. E. (2011). *Competitive advantage of nations: creating and sustaining superior performance.* Simon and Schuster.

Porter, M.E. and Kramer, M.R. (2006), Strategy and society: the link between competitive advantage and corporate social responsibility. *Harvard Business Review*, 84(12), 78–92.

Seuring, S. (2013). A review of modeling approaches for sustainable supply chain management. *Decision Support Systems*, 54(4), 1513–1520.

Seuring, S., & Müller, M. (2008a). From a literature review to a conceptual framework for sustainable supply chain management. *Journal of Cleaner Production*, 16(15), 1699–1710.

Seuring, S., & Müller, M. (2008b). Core issues in sustainable supply chain management–a Delphi study. *Business Strategy and the Environment*, 17(8), 455–466.

United Nations Development Programme (2010) *Productive uses of renewable energy: energy supply chain.*

Wee, H. M., Yang, W. H., Chou, C. W., & Padilan, M. V. (2012). Renewable energy supply chains, performance, application barriers, and strategies for further development. *Renewable and Sustainable Energy Reviews*, 16(8), 5451–5465.

Conclusion

Almost a quarter of a century passed since the world entered into the second millennia. The use of alternative energy sources has been developing relatively fast. At the same time, the total world population, which was only one billion by the 1800s, has increased by about 6.8 billion, reaching 7.8 billion levels in about 220 years. Such a rapidly growing population and constantly developing technologies require more and more energy every day. The high level of energy consumption using nonrenewable sources is negatively affecting environmental quality; as a result, nations prefer to use renewable energy sources. For example, solar energy in the region is sufficient to meet the world's total electricity demand for several years. However, despite the extreme potential in renewable energy, the region does not utilize it efficiently. The underlying reason is in the government's policies. The energy policy of the region that puts greater emphasis on renewable energy sources is tied to the water policy, as the region's scarcity of water and climate conditions result in dependence on energy-intensive methods like air-conditioning and seawater desalination. In this respect, unified energy and water policy planning is a necessity for the region. On the other side, International Energy Agency, in a recent report (2020), assesses the impact of the COVID-19 pandemic on clean energy transition and puts forward the idea that the pandemic is having a major impact on energy systems by curbing investments and threatening to slow the expansion of key clean energy technologies.

The technologies of renewable energy sources do not allow yet to substitute nonrenewable energy sources; therefore, countries continue to be highly dependent on nonrenewable energy sources, which are more efficient in energy production, but are relatively rear and are found only in a few countries and regions. This book focuses on Eastern Europe and the Middle East regions, discussing various aspects related to energy sources of these regions.

In terms of the location of energy sources, Eastern Europe is less lucky compared to the Middle East. Production of nonrenewable energy sources as fossil fuels is heavily dominated by Russia in Eastern Europe, while the Middle East region is widely endowed with various sources of energy. Therefore, to decrease the energy dependence on Russia, Eastern European countries are highly interested in Middle Eastern energy sources, particularly newly discovered. One of the discoveries of high interest in Europe is the EastMed project, which is planned to connect the energy sources of the Eastern Mediterranean region with Italy through Greece. However, unless the political Cyprus issue with Turkey will not be solved, it seems that the project will not start.

In terms of the Cyprus dispute, in most of the statements, Turkey accuses Greek Cypriots of seeing themselves as the only owner of the island and ignoring the rights of the Turkish Cypriots. Turkey emphasizes that the natural wealth of Cyprus should be shared fairly by the two nations that are the co-owners of the island. According to Turkey, Turkish Cypriots and their rights cannot be disregarded, and Turkish Cypriots and Greek Cypriots should decide together on the future of the island. Greece, particularly since 2019, emphasizes Turkey's diplomatic isolation. According to Greece, Turkey is a country that is isolated and constantly losing ground and credibility. Greece portrays itself as a country that respects international law, successful in the diplomatic sphere, and able to establish strong alliances. Greece constantly reiterates its full support and solidarity with the Republic of Cyprus in exercising its sovereign rights in its Exclusive Economic Zone.

More recently, the discovery of natural gas in the Eastern Mediterranean further increased the importance of Turkey in the "Energy Game" of Europe and the Middle East. Countries that are actively involved in new energy source discoveries in the Eastern Mediterranean region, Israel, Greece, and Turkey, have long-lasting disputes, which undermine the possibility of a quick solution to the energy issue. Recent developments in the region, such as the EEZ deal between Turkey and Libya, and the agreement between Israel, Egypt, and Greece, in addition to military actions of France, Greece, and Turkey further deepen the problem rather than using this potential giant infrastructure investment as an opportunity to establish strong relations and solving the regional issues. Besides these developments, as of September 2020, Turkey suspended its drilling activities and gave a chance to Germany to lead an attempt at a peaceful solution to the issue. This, hopefully, will start a new era that is characterized by solutions to never-ending disputes.

Keywords: Eastern Europe, Middle East, Energy Source Discoveries, Energy Dependence, Energy Policy

Index

Aphrodite. *See* Cyprus; Aphrodite gas field
aviation, 12
Azerbaijan, 38–41

Bahrain, 6, 44, 91, 92, 94
barite. *See* nonfuel minerals
Belarus, 6, 12, 30
biofuel, 5, 7, 11, 27
Black Sea, 85
Blue Stream, 17, 37
boron. *See* nonfuel minerals
bromine. *See* nonfuel minerals

carbon: -footprint, 25, 123; -tax, 27–29, 89
carbon dioxide (CO_2) emissions, 11–13, 28, 86, 88, 89, 94, 97, 109
China, 9, 28, 84, 86, 100, 104–7, 109, 112, 119
clay. *See* nonfuel minerals
climate: action program, 25, 129; change, 5, 11, 28, 30, 83–89, 91–92, 95, 100–103, 124; crisis, 99, 111
coal, 5–7, 9–12, 19, 27, 30, 83–85, 88, 100, 112, 117, 120
concentrated solar power (CSW). *See* solar power, concentrated
conflict, 20, 47, 49, 58, 60
Convention of Continental Shelf, 40
COVID–19, 12
Cyprus, 16–20, 37, 39–42, 47–56, 58–64; Aphrodite gas fied, 37, 41, 44, 48

Desertec Project, 111–12
digitalization, 118, 119, 121, 123
diplomatic isolation, 64
Dumat Al Jandal, 106

Eastern Europe, 6–13, 23, 26, 86, 139, 140
EastMed pipeline, 17–19, 41, 72
economic growth, 23–26, 31–32, 87–88, 91–93, 95–97, 102, 112–14
Egypt, 16–17, 21, 39, 48, 50, 57, 60, 63, 101–10
energy: demand, 12, 20, 36, 92–94, 101, 111, 119, 123; efficiency, 23–27, 29–33, 86–89, 109, 117–19, 122, 124–26, 134; importer, 84, 101; -market, 2, 5, 6, 8, 12, 84, 99, 104, 108, 111, 116, 117, 119; nuclear-, 5–11, 19, 59, 83–85, 100, 102, 117, 120, 122, 124; policy, 30, 59, 84, 86, 88, 111; renewable, 5–6, 11, 15, 18, 19, 27, 29, 31, 83–85, 88, 91–97; -security, 19, 21, 25, 36, 37, 39, 44, 86, 95, 101, 111, 117, 118; -sources, 11, 100, 102–11, 116, 124, 133–35; -supply, 5, 8–9, 21, 27, 36, 83, 100, 116–17, 129–37

entrepreneurship, 120, 121
environmental sustainability, 24–26, 29–31, 33, 132, 134–35
exclusive economic zone (EEZ), 39–42, 44–45, 47, 49–52, 60, 64
export, 17, 26, 60, 95–96, 101

feed-in tariffs, 108

gas emissions, 12, 28, 83, 96, 133
GDP. *See* gross domestic product
Gensa Field, 16
geothermal. *See* geothermal; power plants
Greece, 17, 19, 20, 38–45, 47–49, 54, 56–64
Green Economy, 30, 33, 133
greenhouse gas, 12, 24, 25, 28, 83, 92, 96, 100, 133
gross domestic product (GDP), 6, 27, 85, 96, 112

Haifa, 16
HDI. *See* human development; index
health, 24–31, 85, 101
human development, 23–27; -index (HDI), 29–30
hydro, 5, 7, 92, 120; -carbon, 48–51, 53–59, 64; -electricity, 6, 8, 10; -power, 28, 84–85, 93–94, 102, 106, 107, 110

import dependency, 36, 38, 84
INDC. *See* Intended Nationally Determined Contributions
industrialization, 25, 119
Industry 4.0, 118, 126
Intended Nationally Determined Contributions (INDC), 87, 109
Iran, 6–13, 37–39, 89, 91–94, 101–3, 105–7, 109–10, 112; sanctions, 9, 61, 112
Iraq, 6–7, 9–10, 13, 23, 39, 89, 91–92, 94, 101, 103, 107–10
Israel, 16, 17, 21, 37, 39, 41–45, 48, 51–52, 63, 91, 94, 101, 103–5, 107–10; Jerusalem, 39, 41, 43; Leviathan gas field, 16–17, 37, 41, 43–44, 48; Tamar gas field, 16, 37, 41, 48

Jerusalem. *See* Israel
Jordan, 6, 8, 11, 13, 48, 92, 101–12

Karish, 48
Kazakhstan, 23–25, 27, 29–33, 39, 44
Kyoto Protocol, 86, 87, 92

lead. *See* nonfuel minerals
Levant Basin, 15, 16, 20, 92
Leviathan. *See* Israel; Leviathan gas field
Libya, 6, 40–42, 44, 57–58, 89
life expectancy, 24, 27, 29–30

maritime jurisdictions, 50, 52
market, 13, 84, 86, 87, 89, 104, 117, 122–24, 126, 133; electricity-, 96; energy-. *See* energy market: European-, 35–39, 41, 43; hydropower-, 107; natural gas-. *See* natural gas market: wind power-, 105
MDG. *See* Millennium Development Goals
Medgrid Project, 111
Middle East, 1, 2, 5–13, 35, 37, 59, 91–97, 99, 101
Millennium Development Goals, 24–25

natural gas: -consumption, 10, 11, 18–20, 37, 101; demand, 2, 12, 19, 20, 36, 37, 44; discovery, 16, 35, 140; -distribution, 117; -exploration, 50, 53; export, 9, 16, 36; -extraction, 35; -field, 16, 36, 37, 41, 42, 44; import, 11, 18, 19, 84, 94, 101; -industries, 9; -infrastructure, 20; -market, 10, 20, 37, 38, 44, 101, 117; -pipeline, 15, 16, 18, 30, 35, 37, 39, 41, 117;

-prices, 84, 99, 101; -production, 10, 16, 18, 92, 94, 112; -reserves, 6, 7, 10, 16, 28, 37–39, 42, 43, 47, 92–93, 101, 112; -resources, 1, 20, 53, 93; -security, 36, 59; sources, 6, 9, 27, 84, 99, 100; supply, 2, 9, 16, 20, 36–38, 44, 91, 92; transportation, 41, 43
New Energy Triangle, 48
nonfuel minerals, 112
Nord Stream, 17, 37–38
Norway, 18–19, 23, 25, 27–28, 30, 37, 112
nuclear energy. *See*, energy; nuclear

oil: -companies, 54, 84; consumption, 10, 101; crude-, 5, 8, 11, 19; demand, 2, 12; -equivalent, 8, 26; -exploration, 16, 21, 32, 35, 47, 50, 53, 54, 79; -export, 24, 26, 31, 96, 112; -import, 9, 11, 19, 24, 84, 96, 102; -industries, 9; -prices, 84, 99, 101, 112; production, 9, 10, 16, 18, 29, 101, 103; -reserves, 5, 7, 9, 10, 16, 24, 28, 47, 92, 93, 101, 112; -resources, 1, 2, 53, 85, 93, 99, 100; supply, 2, 9, 19, 83, 91, 92, 101

Paris Agreement, 13, 19, 87, 92, 109, 112
photovoltaic, 7, 92, 100
policy, 57; climate-, 86–88; Cyprus-, 63; development-, 84; energy-. *See* energy policy: European-, 86; foreign-, 61; Greek-, 61, 64; -making, 30, 96, 97, 126, 129; public-, 108; Turkish-, 61–63, 87, 94, 96; water-, 111, 139
power plants, 19, 84–85, 116–17, 124; geothermal-, 7, 84–85, 93, 100, 107–8, 110
private: company, 9, 17; interests, 89; sector, 84, 115–18, 121–26
project, 17, 20, 38, 39, 41, 84, 104, 106, 111, 117, 121, 125, 126; EastMed-, 2, 15–21, 140; energy-, 30, 31, 54; hydropower-, 85; natural gas-, 9, 39

Raman Mountain, 35; Qatar, 6, 37, 44, 91–92, 94
renewable energy. *See* energy; renewable
Romania, 6–8, 10
Russia, 6–13, 17–21, 23–25, 27–31, 33–37, 44, 48, 84, 89, 96, 112
Russian Federation. *See* Russia

sanctions. *See* Iran; sanctions
Saudi Arabia, 6–7, 9–12, 23, 91–94, 96, 101, 103–10
security, 10, 49, 55–57, 59, 61, 63, 92, 118; energy-. *See* energy security: natural gas-. *See* natural gas security
SGC. *See* Southern Gas Corridor
shale gas, 99, 112, 124
solar power, 7, 11, 84, 92, 100, 104; concentrated-, 93
Southern Gas Corridor (SGC), 38
start-up, 54–55, 115, 120–23, 126
supply chain, 3, 129–36
sustainable development, 24–25, 27, 85, 102, 111, 132, 135
Sweden, 6, 18

Tamar. *See* Israel; Tamar gas field
TANAP. *See* Trans Anatolian pipeline
Trans Anatolian pipeline (TANAP), 20, 38, 43
Trans Balkan, 17
Trans-European Energy Networks, 36
Turkey, 6, 9, 19–21, 35, 37–45, 47–65, 83–88, 91–92, 94, 101–10, 115–23, 127

UAE, 6–7, 10–12, 48, 91–94, 103–5, 107, 109, 110, 112
Ukraine, 6–12, 30, 36
United Nations, 24, 25, 33, 40, 86, 109
urbanization, 25, 31, 33, 111, 119

war, 41–42, 112
WDI. *See* World Development Indicators
wind turbine, 8, 93, 105, 106
word frequency, 49–51, 58
World Development Indicators (WDI), 94, 98, 114

Yemen, 6, 9, 13, 44, 89, 91–92, 94

zinc. *See* nonfuel minerals
Zohr, 16, 48

About the Editors and Contributors

EDITORS

Natalya Ketenci is a professor in economics at Yeditepe University, Istanbul, where she has been employed for the past sixteen years. She received her PhD in economics from the University of Reading, UK (2003), and an MSc in mathematics from the Kazak State National University, Almaty (1996). At the same time, she is a member of the Centre for Euro-Asian Studies at the University of Reading's Henley Business School. Dr. Ketenci was assisting in the preparation of Transition report 2001: Energy in transition in the European Bank for Reconstruction and Development, London (UK). Her works have been focused on international trade issues in the European Union and emerging countries. Her current research has a focus on energy issues in Turkey and on energy links between European and transition countries. She is one of the editors and authors of the *Turkish-Russian Relations: Prospects and Challenges* book published by Lexington Books in 2019. Her publications include a contribution to such journals as *Energy, Russian Journal of Economics, Empirical Economics, Economic Modeling*, and *Research in Economics*.

Ayşe Sevencan is an assistant professor in economics at Yeditepe University, Istanbul. She received her PhD in economics from Yeditepe University (2010), MA in applied economics from the University of North Carolina (2004), and bachelor's degree in economics from Bilkent University, Ankara (2001). Her research interests include applied macroeconomics, financial markets, and economic growth and development.

CONTRIBUTORS

Alper Altınanahtar received his bachelor degree in public finance from Ankara University, Ankara in 1997. Following his bachelor degree he worked as a research assistant at Faculty of Economics and Administrative Sciences at Mediterranean University, Antalya. In his last year at Mediterranean University, he went to Texas Tech University, Texas, USA, where he received his MA (2001) and PhD (2004) degrees in the field of economics. During his stay at Texas Tech University, he was employed as a teaching assistant, then graduate part-time instructor, and between 2003 and 2005, he was appointed as an assistant professor. Since 2006, Mr. Altınanahtar has been working at the Department of Economics, Yeditepe University. Currently he is an associate professor in economics and appointed as the Vice Dean of the Faculty of Economics and Administrative Sciences. His works have been focused on various health economics topics such as human organ shortage and procurement, socio-economic determinants of suicides and anti-smoking policies and their effects on smoking prevalence.

Barış Gençer Baykan is an assistant professor of public administration at Yeditepe University, Istanbul, where he has been a faculty member since 2013. Baykan completed his PhD in sociology at the University of Kent, UK and MA in political sociology at the University of Paris X/Nanterre. His research interests lie in the area of social movements, anti-GMO movement, the climate movement, and the environmental movement. Baykan teaches social movements, civil society, and global environmental policy. Baykan has authored journal publications and book chapters on the aforementioned topics.

Gizem Alioğlu Çakmak is assistant professor at Yeditepe University, Istanbul. She holds a PhD degree in political science and international relations from the same university. In 2012, she defended her doctoral dissertation entitled "Europeanization of Greek Foreign Policy: Progress, Challenges, and Strategies." In 2011, she attended a Fall School in Athens called "Greece and Turkey in a Changing Europe" which was organized by Sabancı University and the Free University of Berlin, with a grant from the German DAAD foundation. She was a post-doctoral fellow at Panteion University (Athens) (October 2015 to September 2016), where she collaborated with Alexis Heraclides and carried out research on "The Europeanization of minority rights in Greece." Her research interests include Turkish–Greek relations, europeanization, Southeastern Europe, and minorities. She is currently working at Yeditepe University as a full-time assistant professor, teaching Turkish foreign policy, Turkish–Greek relations, and politics and society in the Balkans. She has published numerous articles and chapters in edited volumes. Besides, she is one of the editors of the book from Routledge entitled *Greece and Turkey in Conflict and Cooperation: From Europeanization to de-Europeanization.*

Hatice Kerra Geldi obtained her BS in mathematics from Bogazici University, Istanbul, in 2001. She completed MA in international economics and finance and PhD degree in international economics from Yeditepe University. She is currently working as an assistant professor at the Department of Economics, Yeditepe University. Her research interests include international trade, open economy macroeconomics, exchange rates, and regional integration.

Melih Güner is a fourth-year student at the Department of Political Science and International Relations, Yeditepe University, Istanbul. He has spent six months at the University of Macedonia (Thessaloniki, Greece) as an Erasmus student in 2019. He wrote his graduation thesis on the energy dimension in Turkish–Greek relations. His research interests are Turkish–Greek relations, Southeastern European studies, and energy issues.

Özlem Kunday is a professor at the Department of Business Administration, Yeditepe University, Istanbul. Dr. Kunday holds a BS in applied economics from Gazi University and MBA from Southern Illinois University. She started her PhD courses at United States International University, California, and completed her degree at Yeditepe University. Her research interest is strategic human resource management and entrepreneurship. Since 2018, she is the director of Yeditepe University Management Application and Research Center (MARC).

Özlem Şenvar (PhD in industrial engineering) is an associate professor at the Department of Industrial Engineering, Marmara University, Istanbul. She was official granted (Ref. 2013/327–350) by European Commission for her post-doctoral researches in France. She worked in Logistics and Optimization of industrial Systems of Institute Charles Delaunay, University Technologie Troyes. She has been the author of many peer-reviewed international articles, book chapters, and conference papers. Her research interests involve production and operations management, advanced quality engineering, statistics, machine learning, artificial intelligence, data mining, decision-making, and supply chain management.

Çağrı Levent Uslu was born in Izmir. In 2003, he moved to Lincoln, Nebraska, for a joint PhD program with Yeditepe University and stayed in the United States for two years, where he finished his coursework of the PhD degree. After returning back to Istanbul, he finished his dissertation in 2009. Uslu is employed at Yeditepe University throughout his graduate studies and afterward. His interest areas are macroeconomics, development, international economics, and econometrics. His topics of recent publications are credit rating agencies and their effects on domestic economies, trade openness, development in developing countries, causality between imports, and GDP growth.

Gülfer Vural obtained her BS degree in mathematics from Bogazici University, Istanbul, in 2001. She obtained her MA degree in economics from Bogazici University in 2005. She received her PhD degree in economics from the University of Texas, Austin, in 2010. She works as an assistant professor at the Department of Economics, Istanbul Medeniyet University. Her research interests include macroeconomics, international economics and energy economics. Her recent publications focus on renewable energy, growth nexus for developing and less developed countries.

www.ingramcontent.com/pod-product-compliance
Lightning Source LLC
Chambersburg PA
CBHW051256200926
51612CB00002B/67
9781793644473